$$$

MEGA GIFTS Who gives them, who gets them

Bonus Books, Inc., Chicago

Library of Congress Catalog Card Number:
83-62498

International Standard Book Number:
0-931028-39-6

00 99 98 97 96   10 9 8 7 6

Bonus Books, Inc.
160 East Illinois Street
Chicago, Illinois 60611

Printed in the United States of America

This Book is dedicated to the hundreds of thousands of professionals and volunteers involved in fund raising for great causes, toilers all in the vineyards of philanthropy.

> "Blessed are the money raisers . . .
> for in heaven, they shall stand
> on the right hand of the martyrs."
> —John R. Mott

CONTENTS

PART I

1
THE INCREDIBLE ODYSSEY

*"The Mock Turtle, in a deep hollow tone, said:
'Sit down, and don't speak a word 'til I've fin-
ished.' So they sat down and nobody spoke for
some minutes. Alice thought to herself, 'I don't
see how he can ever finish if he doesn't begin.' "*
—Lewis Carroll
"Alice in Wonderland"

HE WAS WEARING a grey suit. He almost always did. Those who knew him best said he had a closet filled with them. The same grey material. Each meticulously hand sewn and tailored. Each very expensive. Each three piece.

Moses Annenberg was walking down Wall Street in New York City with his son Walter—then a freshman at Peddie, at the time a not too distinguished prep school in New Jersey. It was scorching that August day in 1925, the hottest that oldtimers could remember. In spite of the heat, Moses had each button of his vest and each button of his jacket firmly in place.

There was great affection between these two, father and son. Moses would see to it that the young boy would inherit everything. A not inconsiderable sum. As for Walter, he idolized his father, tried to emulate him in every way possible.

As they walked down Wall Street, Moses reached into his pocket. A couple dollars for a derelict. A hand full of coins for a man begging on the corner. A dollar in the tin cup of a blind man.

"Just remember," Moses admonished his son, "there but for the grace of God go you and I."

Moses Annenberg was raised in abject poverty. He believed that more than anything, his parents were simply unlucky. It wasn't a case of his father not being smart or not working hard. He was uncontrollably unlucky. Moses believed firmly that the deck was stacked against most people and he attempted to impress his son, time after time, after time, that the lucky ones—himself and his son to follow—had a responsibility to help the less fortunate.

They continued their walk down Wall Street, turned up Worth on their way to Broadway. Another beggar, another handful of coins. It wasn't charity. It was raw, impulsive superstition. Moses felt some mild sense of compassion, but mostly he thought that by helping the less fortunate, he could count on his incredible good luck continuing.

It was his compulsion, his motivating philosophy of life. Give, and it comes back to you. Help the poor and the needy. If you do, you will prosper. What seed was planted, consciously or subconsciously, in young Walter's mind?

Even at the time, young Walter Annenberg had a keen sense of pride which made him want the best, whether it was traveling first class, staying at the finest hotel, building a home, or buying a tailored suit. That high level of pride continues to this day. During his high school commencement activities in 1927, the teenage Annenberg donated $17,000 for a new track—the first of countless gifts amounting to many millions of dollars he would bestow on Peddie School. It was his way of making it one of the nation's superior prep schools.

Over the years, his generosity has continued. His support at the University of Pennsylvania alone has totaled about $300 million. Peddie School, however, has remained highest on the list of institutions he watches over most carefully, most paternally—and most generously. He virtually rebuilt the School's campus, assuring new dormitories, a library, a gymnasium, and a planetarium. There was one brief point when he closed the wellspring of donations because his gifts had resulted in others taking for granted the idea that Annenberg would always pick up the tab. A "let Walter do it" syndrome permeated the campus and the graduates. He remains, however, a sentimental graduate, full of tender remembrances of his days at Peddie. Fond memories and nostalgic recollections still bring tears to his eyes when he thinks back.

When Annenberg returned to the States after serving as Ambassador to the Court of St. James, under President Nixon, he promptly established a Child Day Care Center at the Desert Hospital in Palm Springs, California. This was the first of many gifts to this hospital. Like many of his gifts, the factor which motivated him was his strong personal determination that there was a need for his money. The purpose of the Center was to provide aid and comfort to abused children, a problem he became acutely aware of only shortly before he left his Embassy post. He read a London paper one day and came across an article about a little girl who had been physically harmed by her father. It was unthinkable to Annenberg that a parent could really do such a thing, so he went to the hospital to see for himself and to talk with the child. It was true. She had been battered, abused, molested. Her whole body was covered with burns from a cigarette. ''When I saw what had been done to her, I felt sick and knew that I had to do something to help these children.''

Walter Annenberg is one of the great benefactors of this nation. His recent gift of $150 million for a communications complex is considered to be the largest single private donation ever given by a living person.

Who can be certain of the impetus which motivates this generosity. Likely, Walter Annenberg himself cannot be certain. Recognition and tribute? Hardly likely— he is a very private man and has almost always eschewed any identification with his gifts. A great commitment to the needs and concerns of the needy? Probably not—the greatest majority of his gifts have been for special programs and the general good of mankind, but not for the oppressed and needy. Superstition, to guarantee his continued good luck? It is hard to say and perhaps even Walter Annenberg cannot unlock the answer to the puzzle.

*   *   *   *   *

The rise of Julius Rosenwald's fortunes from meager resources to behemoth riches is a Horatio Alger story of extraordinary proportions, one of the most dramatic in the nation's history. It was by sheer accident that he became a partner and major stockholder in Sears, Roebuck. Pure serendipity. The fact that he quickly bought out his brother-in-law for a pittance in order to take control of the company is another matter. But that is a story to be told in a different setting.

It was his genius which built the company, and his fortunes grew from virtually nothing to an estimated $600 million. All this in just seven years. And when a dollar was worth closer to a dollar!

He was a strange mixture, Julius Rosenwald was. His personal spending habits were extraordinary. He thought nothing, for instance, of building tennis courts on the grounds of his baronial home in a suburb of North Shore Chicago. He refused, however, to buy tennis balls. That was wasteful!

Odd as his spending habits were, he loved giving money away. It was his passion. In his case, the recipients were the poor and his special concern was for the deplorable condition and plight of young blacks, particularly in the South. He began building what became known as "Rosenwald Schools." All told, there were over 5,000 schools, shops, and housing units which were scattered all over the Southern states. A hundred YMCAs were built for black people. There was scholarship assistance and fellowships. All for black people and all segregated. But this was the pattern of the time.

What is unusual about his giving is that it followed what could only be considered an unpopular course. It was totally unlike the other great Jewish philanthropists —Schiff, Warburg, Kahn—who gave to more conventional institutions: the museums, the medical centers, the "proper and approved" institutions. In the case of Rosenwald, he insisted that his name be attached to his gifts. He confessed that he wanted immortality.

Some wags claim that Rosenwald was not unmindful of the fact that his growing fortunes were related directly to black people's ability to buy goods from those exciting, new Sears catalogues. As their ability to pay for merchandise grew, Rosenwald prospered. What truly motivated his giving? A selfishness? An over-expanded ego? Or a strong commitment to help the needy? Likely all of these factors and more.

*   *   *   *   *

John Davison Rockefeller was a man in a hurry. He made his first million dollars at age 23. Those who knew him best, from both sides of the table, claim that from his modest beginnings at the lowest rung of the financial ladder, he had an absolute magnet-affinity for making money. In his lifetime, he gave away more than any other individual. It is hard to determine precisely the exact amount, but it is likely in excess of $600 million.

Where was the seed planted? What motivating force drove him to his outreach to people?

He was a tiger. Even as a teenager when his earnings were meager—and at times he was virtually penniless— he gave away one-tenth of his income.

His pattern was established. But some of his closest associates say that something extraordinary happened about the time he made his first magic million. The report from a medical examination indicated serious problems. The young millionaire was desperately ill. The doctor recommended acidulated milk and crackers, a diet he adhered to for the next seven decades of his life. The diet also perhaps explains his typically unpleasant appearance, or even possibly his longevity.

It was at this point in his life that John D. Rockefeller became a committed giver. An unrelenting giver. He even had his servant fill his pockets each morning with fifty new dimes, to be presented to strangers as he walked to work. On special occasions, the dimes were changed to silver dollars.

His giving was ceaseless, for a variety of causes and to countless institutions and organizations. Was this simply a continuation of a life-long habit? Was there perhaps a secret covenant made with his God, a pact made after hearing his doctor's report?

* * * * *

What motivates large gifts? What are the psychological factors, the pressures, the social imperatives that drive men and women to make gifts of consequential size? Gifts of a million dollars or more.

The answer is complex, a puzzle. The plain fact is that probably no single factor is the overriding determinant in making the decision. It is more likely a combination of feelings, timing, past giving experience, and the motivation and exigency of the moment. Perhaps sheer serendipity. Addison L. Winship II, the very able and effective vice president of Dartmouth College, says, "Answers will vary from institution to institution . . . seldom does one reason predominate or prevail. It is a combination of many factors."

A number of really fine books have been published on fund raising. Not a long list, but a respectable one. Almost all deal with the mechanics of fund raising, the "nuts and bolts" of organizing a development office or structuring a campaign. They are helpful, especially to the beginner. In an excellent book just published, a review of the table of contents reveals the ubiquitous subjects: The Fundamentals. Procedures. Professional Staff. Public Relations. Communications and Special Events. Financial and Gift-Control Procedures. Volunteers. Charts and Forms. Data Processing. Deferred Gifts and Bequests. Federal Grantsmanship. For some, this is indispensable reference material. Add it to your library shelf. (*Tested Ways to Successful Fund Raising,* George A. Brakeley, Jr. AMACOM Publishing. 1982.)

What does not exist in the field is material which describes how to make it happen. How do you really secure a large gift? There's precious little, virtually nothing, that deals with the question of what motivates people to give. And that, after all, is what it is really about. That's the nub of it. There is very little that penetrates into the deep emotional psyche of a large donor. The existing books have a piece of a chapter here, a reference there, a tidbit hidden in the middle of a paragraph. Very few gems, indeed, and the mining through an entire book isn't always worth the discovery.

I read the books. Like other professionals and volunteers, I understand how to develop a prospect list, how to acknowledge a gift, how to properly train a worker, how many prospects a volunteer can adequately cover. But the overriding, quintessential question remains. How do you capture a large gift? That's really the heart of a fund raising program. The mechanics are the necessary day-to-day indications of a properly managed fund raising office, but the large gift—that is the very heartbeat.

Why does Alex Spanos, a brilliant West Coast apartment builder, give away millions to a variety of institutions, but refuse to give to one local organization? Why did he give $250,000 recently to a museum he had never visited and in response to a telephone call from someone he did not really know? Why did Marianne Mori give over a million dollars to the esoteric and little known Thesaurus Linguae Graecae program at the University of California? What prompted Arthur Rubloff to give $5 million to a university he never attended?

Dmitri George recently gave $1 million to a Midwest hospital. He says: "Why did I give away that much. Well, first of all, we had the money to give. That's where you start!" Not everyone has the ability to make a large gift, but an extraordinary number of people do have the financial resources. Of those who do, not every one gives. How do you find the "right button"? And when you do, how do you most effectively push it? Solving this riddle has led me on an incredible odyssey.

I make you a promise. This book will deal directly with the factors which have motivated a number of people to give gifts of a million dollars and more. The professional and even the uninitiated volunteer will find much here which physicians in a medical report normally call "unexceptional." Just plain common sense elements. Much here may annoy you. Some items may surprise you. Some sections may confirm what you already thought. And some findings will be in direct opposition to some of the hoary verities of fund raising. I have practiced and lived some of the principles which I now find are not valid. The evidence is so clear that it has made a believer, a convert out of me.

What motivates people to make large gifts is in this book. Much of it in the words of the people who actually made the mega gift. Their feelings. Their attitudes. The reasons which brought them to that special decision.

Join me on this odyssey, but I admonish you—keep an open mind. Much of what you are about to read will shatter some of the principles which have been held dear to the hearts of those of us who have been in the field a long time.

Let us begin the journey. Like Alice's White Rabbit, putting on his spectacles: " 'Where shall I begin please, Your Majesty?' The King looked at him very gravely and replied. 'Begin at the beginning . . . and go on 'til you come to the end . . . then stop.' " Let us begin by probing the status of fund raising in today's world. The journey begins.

2
GETTING YOUR SHARE

"The future isn't what it used to be!"

THIS PAST YEAR, $60.39 billion was given to all causes by all sources. Of this amount, 89.7 per cent of all the money which was given was donated by men and women, and only nine per cent of that came from bequests.

That means that nearly 81¢ out of every dollar that was given to a philanthropic endeavor was provided by living people. Corporations and foundations will not save our not-for-profit institutions and organizations. They have not in the past. They will not in the future. Men and women, properly motivated and giving from personal resources will make the difference.

Philanthropy is as old as time. It traces its ancestry to the city-state of Athens, and seven centuries before that to the Egyptian Pharaohs who established ''bequests'' to support religious rites. It was even prevalent and a tradition during the period of the Roman Empire. And then, it was most often a matter of civic pride.

The Young Pliny, for example, discovering that the children in his native town of Como had to go to school in Milan because Como had no teacher for them, put up a third of the expense of hiring an instructor, stipulating that his fellow townsmen must raise the rest. The first challenge gift on record! ''I would have a man generous to his country, his neighbors, his kindred, his friends, and most of all his poor friends. Not like some who are the most lavish with those who are able to give most to them.''

During his lifetime, Pliny also gave 30,000 sesterces a year from the rentals of his lands to the support of Como's lower-class children. More than that, he built for his native city a municipal library and provided for its upkeep. On his death, he left a great sum of money for the support of 100 freedmen who had been his slaves, adding that after their deaths the income was to be used to provide an annual banquet for the people. Throughout the Empire, cities were growing rich and foundations were being established to do for other communities what Pliny had done for Como.

The Old Testament is replete with notations regarding philanthropy and duty. In Old Testament times, the people are admonished ''. . . (Where the Lord designates) you shall come and bring your whole-offerings and sacrifices, your tithes and contributions, your vows and free-will offerings, and the first born of your herds and flocks.'' Deuteronomy 12:6.

* * * * *

In 1913, when the first federal income tax act was passed in this country, there were dire predictions of the demise of philanthropy. And in each of the recent years when there has been a major reform in the tax provisions —1969, 1976, and 1981—the same voices of doom persisted. But philanthropy continues to grow, year after year, each succeeding one larger in total volume than the year before.

But it's not getting easier. It is getting more difficult, more bewildering. More confounding. As E. B. White noted: ''I see a great future for complexity.''

The competition for the contribution dollar is fierce. The philanthropic pie gets larger and larger with each succeeding year. But there is evidence that the successful organization becomes more successful. The institutions that do not do well will do even less well. There is reason to believe that only a Yale University could surpass its recent $370 million objective. Benjamin Franklin could have been describing Yale when he wrote: ''God who made thee mighty, make thee mightier yet.''

Giving is not a democratic procedure. Small contributors are important because they provide a broad base of giving and produce an important part of the project that is necessary;. But in fund raising, ''the rule of thirds'' prevails. This verity remains essentially unchallenged, continues to persist, and is true of almost every campaign. One third of your money comes from about your top ten donors, and the next third from about the following one hundred donors. This is the gospel of fund raising which is virtually inviolate. Another formula which continues to be valid is that 80 per cent of the money in a campaign program comes from 20 per cent of the donors.

In the mid-1970s, Yale met its $370 million goal by surpassing its objective by $4 million. At that level, what's $4 million one way or the other? In this campaign, the rule of thirds governed again. About one-third of the money came from the top ten gifts. Harvard is currently engaged in a campaign for $350 million. They have projected that 75 per cent of the drive's gifts will come from 1 per cent of all donors. And even in Missoula, Montana, in the campaign just completed for St. Patrick Hospital, one-third of the money came from the top ten donors. The rule of thirds can be counted on in campaign after campaign after campaign.

This underlines the critical significance of individual giving. Large gifts. Gifts of monumental consequence.

* * * * *

For the conventional institution, it is an unconventional time! We live in a society that creates problems faster than it can solve them. It is possible that in the next decade, 25 per cent of the population will be Hispanic or black and in all likelihood, Hispanics will outnumber the blacks. The exodus to the Sun Belt States will continue in increasing number. The old, large cities, plagued by shivering cold winters, are expected to continue to lose people. In the latest census, America's ten largest cities include four in the Sun Belt and in the next ten years, the group will jump to six.

We'll see some movement back into the large city, but the suburban lifestyle will continue to be the major momentum of the American mainstream. The population will grow older, and there will be an ever-increasing number of smaller households.

The "haves" will have more, and the "have-nots," less. It is estimated that in only a few years, 30 per cent of the population will be members of households receiving under $10,000 a year. Sheer survival will be the question.

The demographic factors are clear. Lay those against the sociological elements that institutions must face. If they are like most, their constituencies are better educated and more demanding. There is the ascendancy of the consumer.

There is less sense of neighborhood, less sense of civic pride and responsibility. There is the general erosion of the family unit. There is a blurring of sex roles.

There is an increase of leisure time, but less money to spend on it. There is less prestige for the physician and much more concern for embracing wellness instead of treating disease. It is a time of health, nutrition, exercise. Health is the order of the day, and 23 per cent of the adult population engages in some sort of vigorous exercise at least three times a week.

Lord Melblourne said about historian Macaulay: "I wish I could be as certain of anything as Macaulay is about everything." In today's world, one thing that is certain is uncertainty. Institutions will require more and more funds from the private sector. There is ample evidence that those that will succeed will be the courageous, the innovative, the aggressive. What will be required is creative and strategic planning—a do-something attitude that expects the impossible, and achieves it.

Organizations and institutions are in the business of serving people, but an explosion is taking place. Scientific and technical information increases by 13 per cent a year, which means it doubles every five and a half years. And it is projected that this rate will jump to 40 per cent a year because of new and more powerful information systems. It is an era of computer kit-and-kaboodle and micro-everything. New ideas in confrontation with the old.

Arthur C. Clarke says that when a distinguished but elderly scientist says that something is possible, he is always right. When the scientist states that something is impossible, he is probably wrong. And Clarke considers anyone over thirty years of age as elderly. Without question, to say "impossible" in today's world always puts you on the losing side.

America is converting from an industrial-based economy to one which is geared to the production and processing of information. Over 60 per cent of the work force is involved in the handling of information; only 13 per cent is still engaged in manufacturing. The Futurologists tell us that we can not depend on the old reliable indicators such as the Dow-Jones Industrial Average—it will no longer reflect the economy's true vigor. Most significantly, for every high-technology advance, there is an equal and opposite social reaction. Technology jumps forward in quantum leaps, much faster than the ability of people to adjust to it.

All of this can be terrifying and confounding to an organization whose mission is serving people. The Futurologists claim that we are moving into a "new" America, post-industrial, scientifically, and technologically based on an "information" society. But this cannot save us if we are not equipped for it. The Carnegie Council of Policy Studies in Higher Education says: ". . . about one-third of youth is ill-educated, ill-employed and ill-equipped to make their way in American society." There is a staggering agenda.

* * * * *

No matter who occupies the chair in the White House, less government funds will be available for your organization. There is less interest on the part of laymen to serve your organization. Leadership on the board will have to be won—there will be more competition for board members and less willingness to serve. *Fortune* magazine conducted a study recently to determine why men and women were unwilling today to serve on boards. There were four major reasons: 1) people are much more concerned about the liability problems which now arise with board membership; 2) they are no longer willing to give the time that is required; 3) it is no longer considered an honor to serve on a board; and 4) there is less interest in getting involved in anything other than family and business. The *Fortune* survey was conducted among the top 400 corporations in the country regarding corporate board membership. The same reasons for disinclination to serve on boards could be stated for the not-for-profits.

Less discretionary funds will be available for organizations and operating costs will become increasingly more expensive. In most situations, it costs 18 per cent more each year just to stay even. And for those organizations with buildings and facilities, energy costs can eat that up in one gulp during a difficult winter. Small colleges in New England, for instance, are facing a losing battle regarding the energy dilemma.

There is a tendency toward fewer organizations. The small and the weak will be merged with larger ones. Human and social service will become more sophisticated. And more expensive. Total public disclosure will be required. These are not times for the amateur or for the weak-of-heart.

It is an era of change. Unprecedented in our history. Too many institutions are like the man driving on a busy Los Angeles freeway who says to his wife: "Don't worry that we're lost—we're making good time." There will be no place for the organization that is "making good time." Everything will depend on knowing where you are going. Otherwise, you have made a commitment to drift.

Grade schools across the country still have that special period called recess. During one such recess, a first grader said to another: "Do you feel our scientists have sufficiently probed the spheres of stratospheric navigation in such a way to appear to permit tertiary penetration of ozonic cyclical thrust to increase velocity and terminal soundings?" The other first grader replied: "I am not particularly aware nor acutely knowledgeable about that specific phase of technological empiricism, but I do have empirical concern about the transfer of travel and energy as it relates to omega levels of acceleration." Just then, the bell sounded, ending recess. The one first grader said: "Now we have to go in and string those damn beads again!" This is no time for organizations to be stringing beads.

There are many problems. And many opportunities. The president of General Electric recently said: "At our company, we never talk about problems, we only talk about opportunities. But sometimes, there are more opportunities than we really care to handle."

These are indeed grave times, difficult times, complex times, for your institution. But there have never been more opportunities. And there has never been a more exciting time to be in the business of fund raising. It will require you to think smarter, work harder, plan bolder, and commit yourself with greater fervor and missionary zeal to the needs of your institution. For many, philanthropy will be the answer. Increased giving from the private sector will be the lifeline. And most important of all will be the generation of large gifts. Really large gifts.

Large gifts, they are there for your organization. Men and women, waiting to be asked. Men and women, waiting for the right program, the proper motivation, the excitement and exhilaration of sharing in a great adventure. The times are difficult but as Mark Twain said, commenting on Wagner's music: "It isn't as bad as it sounds."

3
THE BUCK STARTS WITH THE BOARD

"Every profession is a conspiracy against the laity."

—*Shaw*

W*ALTER* A. H*AAS*, J*R.* *for years headed what is considered the world's most successful garment manufacturer, Levi Strauss & Co. The company was founded by his great-granduncle. He is a recognized leader in the business community, locally and internationally. He is a strong advocate of volunteerism and has played an extremely vital volunteer role his entire adult life.*

An active giver in the Jewish community, Mr. Haas has been equally generous to a wide range of organizations and institutions. His greatest enthusiasm and support, however, is reserved for the University of California, Berkeley, where he graduated in 1937.

Mr. Haas makes it clear that serving on the board of directors of an organization carries with it a financial responsibility. "Someone like me should not serve on a board without supporting it financially. I think that every board member should give. I don't think you can ask others for money unless you've given yourself. Of course, some people are good board members because they give money, others are better at giving time, and others their special experience. But I still think that giving should be a prerequisite to board membership. It's just like being on the board of a corporation, you should own a few shares of stock."

Walter Haas is willing to give his time and resources where his commitment is. He feels strongly that the private sector carries a responsibility to address the problems and opportunities of the countless non-profit organizations. He feels, too, the need for the private sector to be much more innovative and efficient in its giving.

Serving on the board of an organization is a high calling and implies a major responsibility and commitment. Brown University's former president Henry Wriston originated the three venerable "W's" years ago. They are just as relevant today. Perhaps more so. He established for his trustees three criteria—work, wealth, and wisdom. Every institutional administrator fervently longs for trustees who can bring a matched set of all three of the "W's." Two of the three should be mandatory. And if a trustee brings only one "W," the chances are fairly certain that his or her effectiveness will be severely limited. Woe to the organization with a board comprised of one "W's".

It was interesting that among the group I interviewed, service on a board was rated to be an insignificant factor in determining their major gift to the institution. It's interesting for while they may think they feel that way, in most cases they happen to serve as a trustee of the institution where they made their $1 million gift. Louise M. Davies makes no bones about it. She recently gave the largest single gift by a living person in the history of San Francisco. It was the gift which provided the great thrust in constructing the new, magnificent performing arts center in the city. Mrs. Davies says: "If you serve on the board, you're expected to give. You shouldn't be a director or a trustee unless you are prepared to make a gift. If you're not, get out of the way so somebody else can serve." Last year twenty out of thirty persons who gave $1 million gifts were on the board of directors of the recipient institution.

There can be no question about the importance of board membership and direct involvement in the making of a gift. Harold J. Seymour, the great doyen of fund raising, calls it "the pride of association." Membership on a board builds a loyalty and a favorable attitude toward the institution, its activities, and its staff. And very likely what triggers it most effectively into action, more dramatically than anything else, is actual participation in the program. More than just attending meetings and eating countless chicken a la king dinners, it involves acceptance of real responsibility for committee work. Frances Mason wrote a fascinating monograph twenty-five years ago which is just as relevant today. In her piece, "The American Woman—A Thoughtful Donor,'' she says that membership on a board was found in every instance where loyalty of the donor had been early wooed, won, and kept by the beneficiary. "In all instances, the size of the donor's gift increased with the growth of the donor's personal involvement with the organization's problems and progress."

It is a truism that dollars follow commitment. And commitment follows involvement.

One institutional director observed, but only in half-jest, the three "B's" of board membership: the never-ending discussion of budget, buildings, and baloney! But it obviously pays off.

When George Pardee was quite young, his father's construction business went bankrupt. George and his brother went into the business, picked up where their father left off, and built the new firm into one of the largest development enterprises in Southern California. The Pardees' reputation is impeccable. They recently sold the firm to the Weyerhauser Company. George Pardee is semi-retired but is as active and vital as ever, possibly more so. He continues to serve on the National Council of the Boy Scouts of America (BSA) and a number of the other important national and local boards, but BSA is a consuming interest—an outgrowth of his scouting days as a youngster. He is extremely generous and choses his philanthropy and his board memberships carefully.

Mr. Pardee says: "Being on the board of an organization is a major factor in my making a gift. When you are involved in board leadership it has a price tag. The first person you have to solicit is yourself. I've got to give to anything I'm involved in. I know that when I tell a group that I am willing to serve on its board, that means that I have a responsibility to help provide for its needs. That's part of the responsibility you take on.''

Very few are fooled by a sudden request to serve on a board. Most often, it means a gift. Remember the three ''W's''! But few large donors are surprised or offended. Alex Spanos flashes enthusiasm easily, in this case for the president of the University on whose board he sits. ''The president of the University is an inspiring person. And plenty smart. He put me on the board of regents and that was important to me. I was giving to the University before then but I have certainly done better since being on the board. I wanted to resign later because I just don't have time for meetings, but they won't let me. And that's plenty smart also.''

W. Clement Stone is the guru of the Positive Mental Attitude. He invented it. He lives it. He breathes it. He is an immensely wealthy man, at one time featured in Fortune *magazine as one of the ten wealthiest in the country. Estimates are that his assets are somewhere in the range of $600 million. Stone admits to only $500 million. He has given at least $100 million away since he started his program of benevolence. He is generous, sometimes wildly so. But always with great compassion. He is the true American Horatio Alger, from abject poverty to the building of an empire. A conversation with him is always exciting, enlightening, and full of surprises.*

To those who do not know him well, the word that most closely characterizes him is ''flamboyant''. The ever present cigar. (In fact, immediately before our altercation with Castro's Cuba, Stone purchased three whole warehouses of his favorite cigar.) The oversized bowtie. The pencil-thin mustache. The at times strained drama in his voice. Underneath it all, there is one of the most sensitive and caring men God ever made.

There are few greater proponents of volunteerism and board service than W. Clement Stone. And he backs up his strong commitment with major gifts. Stone says: "Volunteers and service on a board are significant factors to me. I believe it is our American way of life. I have done a great deal to help support the cause of volunteerism. I only serve on a board when I am willing to get involved in a project and want other people to get involved, also. I don't mind going after people in asking them to join me in something that is really important."

Robert Saligman is a Philadelphia developer and a generous donor. "Being on the board of an organization helps motivate me in making a large gift. There is no question about it, it makes me feel a stronger responsibility. What others on the board do weighs heavily on my own thinking regarding a gift. You cannot serve on the board of an organization and avoid your financial responsibility. If you are not going to make a gift, up to the very limit of your capability, then you should get off the board."

The evidence is clear. Serving on the board of an organization provides great incentive for major giving. A time-tested verity is that the more people know about you, the better they love you! Financial commitment follows personal and direct involvement. Major gifts come from those who know you best of all.

But it's not that easy. How do you recruit, keep, and inspire board members? The million dollar donors give major credit to staff leadership. In fact, they rated this as the third most important factor which motivated their million dollar gifts.

*   *   *   *   *

Staff leadership is a critical and key issue. A strong staff breathes life and vitality into an organization. Where there is momentum and courageous planning, you find a strong executive staff person. Strong staff attracts strong board leadership. One begets the other. Strong staff is professionally challenged and stimulated by strong board leadership. Thrives on it! Sparks ignite. It's synergy.

Where you find a vital, dynamic institution, you find strong staff. A financially sound institution is led by strong staff. A staff which pursues its objectives with ardor and aggressiveness, with fervor and single mindedness.

The weak institution, the financially unstable institution, is most often led by weak and ineffective staff. Weak and ineffective staff most often attract weak and ineffective board members. Highly powered, decisive, influential men and women are not inspired by weak staff.

Strong boards hire strong staff. These organizations raise money. Weak boards most often hire weak staff. These organizations do not raise money.

The strong get stronger. Success succeeds. The weak will not survive.

Clement Stone is one who puts major importance on the management staff. Before making a gift, he looks first to see that the organization is properly staffed. ''If an organization needs your help, you've got to help them. I think the managment is the most important thing. Management makes the difference. I won't give to a program unless I feel it can be properly managed.''

Clement Stone is a fascinating giver! There appears to be no rhyme or reason to the pattern of his philanthropy. But look closer. He consistently bets on people. If he doesn't have full confidence and trust in the chief staff person, the organization is most likely not to get a gift. On the other hand, if there is an attraction, an affinity, a burst of electricity which sends off sparks—the organization is likely to receive a gift. A large gift! Clement Stone gives to a wide range of interests that many of the more conventional and visible donors eschew. The thread which binds this divergent group of beneficiaries is his unshakable belief in professional leadership. I have often thought it would be fascinating to bring together in a small room—no, it would require a large room—the men who have reason to be grateful for the generosity of Clement Stone: Richard Nixon, Norman Vincent Peale, Dr. Benjamin Cohen of the Boston Evening Clinic, Dr. Robert Schuller, the dynamic founder and senior minister of the Crystal Cathedral in Garden Grove, California—and at least a hundred more.

Interlochen is now considered one of the important summer music camps in the nation. It would not be unfair to say that before Clement Stone got involved in the program, it didn't really amount to very much. It was virtually unknown. He breathed life into it, and gave millions of dollars. He was just as generous with his time. He is known as one of the most effective salesmen in the country and more than a few friends and businessmen found themselves on the giving-end of a solicitation call by Stone. Today, largely through his efforts, Interlochen is one of the country's great music centers. In some ways, he did it almost single-handedly, although he was able to recruit a number of others to join him. No one really knows for certain what really turned him on. From where did that whirlwind of activity and money come? Surprisingly, music is not his greatest interest, not by far. What did create the motive and inspiration for his dedication? No one knows for certain. I think I do. Clement Stone told me: "It was the dynamic leadership and vision of the staff—that's what got me going and that's what kept me interested."

Dr. Kenneth Chorley is considered to be the genius behind Colonial Williamsburg. You don't recognize the name? Chorley was the chief executive staff person Rockefeller hired to head the planning and implement the program for Colonial Williamsburg. It was the Rockefeller millions that made it possible, and it was the Chorley inspiration and encouragement which made it happen. Rockefeller says: "I had the dream but Ken Chorley gave me the inspiration. He continually kept the vision alive for me. The money itself would have meant nothing without the leadership he provided."

Cyril Magnin is the acknowledged "Mr. San Francisco." He is one of the city's greatest leaders and benefactors. Before making a gift, he studies the organization carefully. "The financial stability of an organization is important to me. But I relate this directly to the staff leadership and the people who run the organization. If I believe in the staff, I know that everything else is in order."

Magnin goes on to say that: "Staff leadership of an organization means everything to me. I've got to believe in the staff and know that the organization is being managed properly. There is one major group in the city I was instrumental in bringing to San Francisco. That was about fifteen years ago. During that time, I supported it financially and served on its board. In fact, I supported it quite heavily. I did everything I could to make it successful. But as soon as I lost respect for the director, when I felt that he was no longer doing what needed to be done, I gave it up, just like that. I gave up my child! Maybe I was wrong. Maybe I was right. But that's exactly how I felt. There was no way I could continue supporting an organization in which I did not have total respect and regard for the staff."

Dorothy Simmerly is not her real name. She was one of three I interviewed who asked that I not identify her. She is a curious and extraordinary mix of Golda Meier and Auntie Mame. Her family was immensely wealthy and influential and, at one time, she was the chief executive officer of one of the family's interests, a multi-million dollar enterprise. She is now extremely active in a variety of businesses and investment ventures in the southwest.

Dorothy Simmerly is a two-fisted businesswoman, and a two-fisted donor. Her giving is generous. And thoughtful. And calculated. "I am probably not as concerned about the staff leadership of an institution as others are. I know that this can be changed. If I make a large gift to an organization I would expect to have some influence if change really was necessary."

Arthur Rubloff feels strongly: "If you haven't got the

right staff and the right management, you've got nothing. I would not support an institution that didn't have an effective staff. To me, it's everything. It's what I look for first of all. I know that if we have the right staff, we can accomplish anything.''

Virginia Piper gives away millions. Her philanthropy is almost always emotional and spontaneous. But she feels strongly about the role of the staff. ''When I evaluate a gift to an organization, I feel the management has to be outstanding. I have to believe in them. And one follows the other—if there's a good manager, there's always a good and strong board. Always. I'm terribly concerned about how an institution is managed. I feel that it is possibly one of the greatest factors I consider when deciding to give. It has got to be a management that you have faith in and one which has integrity.''

''It's not hard to explain,'' says Mrs. William Deree. The Derees recently gave $1.5 million to the American College of Greece. William Deree had the financial resources to make the gift. His wife, Roberta, provided the inspiration and encouragement which made the gift finally possible. William Deree was passionately Greek. That helps explain his gift to an institution with a Greek heritage. But why to the American College? Why not to the Greek Orthodox Church? Or the Greek Welfare Foundation? Or St. Basil's Academy? Or Hellenic College? He was on the board or a leader in each one of these organizations. The key was the staff leadership, the president of the College. Roberta Deree says: ''Bill has this tremendous regard for the president. The respect finally grew into a personal friendship and the emotions got quite mixed. It is hard to know where respect begins and friendship ends. But there is also the sense of integrity, the feeling that the president is a strong captain of a ship, and he knows where he is going. I know that the gift finally went to the College for that reason.''

George Pardee says it all. ''The staff leadership of the organization is extremely important. I consider it one of the most important factors. If I am turned off for any reason or don't have the kind of confidence in the staff that I think should be there, I just won't give. If I feel good about the staff and I have confidence in them, I can be counted on to do just about anything.''

When staff leadership is right, key volunteers can always be counted on to follow. The president of the college, the administrator of the hospital, the executive director of the organization—their roles are critical. The most effective among this group dream the big, bold dreams. The exciting, new visions. They are the builders. The designers. They are intolerant of status quo. There is often a tendency which can best be described as an inner explosion. Volunteers will follow this kind of leadership with critical but loving devotion and commitment. And they will give to this kind of leadership.

Do men and women serve on a board of an organization because they are large donors? Or are they large donors because they serve on the board? Or, as is most likely the case, do they serve on the board of an institution because of unswerving faith and respect in its chief executive officer? It is fair to say that really large gifts are not made to institutions where there is not proper regard for the staff. Conversely, it is true that of the people I interviewed, the million dollar gifts were made to institutions and organizations where there was an unbreakable bond of regard and respect between the donor and the institution's chief staff person. And this was true in gift after gift after gift. There was not one exception.

4
WHY PEOPLE GIVE

He gives only worthless gold
Who gives from a sense of duty.
—James Russell Lowell

PEOPLE DO NOT GIVE because there is a need. Countless thousands of organizations and institutions have great needs. Overwhelming financial problems. A facility that simply must be renovated, equipment that must be purchased, a roof that must be replaced.

But donors run away from "needs." They hide from the institution that is not financially stable. Large donors give to heroic, exciting programs rather than to needy institutions. Harold J. Seymour says: "The case must catch the eye, warm the heart, and stir the mind." It is trite, but true: an institution must exhibit the audacity and power of an idea whose time has come.

Alex Spanos tells how a hospital approached him to give a million dollars, and for that they would name the alcohol treatment center after him. But it had absolutely no appeal at all. "I know there is a need, especially in that particular area. But for one thing, I don't drink. That kind of a center just has no meaning to me. I do respect the hospital, however, so I gave them $250,000 toward the project and said that they should name the center for Betty Ford. That's what they did, and they raised a lot of money for it. I never give because I think there is a need. There are lots of needs. I give because it's a program I'm interested in and I think I can make a real difference."

It's not easy growing up in the same household with one of Texas's most powerful and influential leaders. Amon Carter, Jr. carried that burden throughout his life. His father, publisher of the formidable Fort Worth newspaper, exerted virtually omnipotent control over everything that happened in the state, political and otherwise. Ben Johnson observed 300 years ago: "Greatness of the name in the father overwhelms the son, they stand too near one another. The shadow kills the growth." Amon, Jr. never really had the influence of his father. It was inevitable. It was a different era. But he was kindly and had a compassionate spirit. He was involved in many Fort Worth programs, and state and national boards. During World War II, he was a prisoner of war and he never forgot the concerned—almost tender—treatment he received from a YMCA director. He gave generously to countless organizations and projects, but nothing was closer to his heart than the YMCA. He repaid his prisoner of war debt many times over to his local YMCA.

Amon Carter, Jr. talks about how he is driven by challenges. ''I give to a program only when I can see some important benefits. People have got to see how they can share in important opportunities. It's a job—how do you pick out of a thousand different organizations whether you'll make a gift? I give heavily to the YMCA, for instance, because I know how important it is and what a great service it provides. I can attest to that from my own experience.''

Robert Saligman says that it is more than just the need that gets to him. There is no end to the organizations with financial needs. When he sees that something has to be done and that there is a great opportunity for him specifically to play an important and particular role, he is inclined to make a gift.

*   *   *   *   *

Large donors feel that giving money away is often bewildering, enigmatic, and an awesome responsibility. All of them take their giving seriously.

And, it is quite clear, there isn't any single reason why people give. My interviewing shows evidence that in most cases, the donor isn't quite certain what was the greatest incentive. As in most human behavior, the action that finally motivates giving is puzzling, complex, and often confluent. The act of making a large gift is uncommonly complicated.

According to the late Harry Golden, one of the chief differences between Jewish and Gentile giving is that

Jews will give the big money while they live, Gentiles when they die. The Jew, says Golden, wants to enjoy the prestige and gratitude. One other major difference—the Jew feels that giving is an ingrained duty.

Among the Jews, there does appear to be a sense of responsibility and duty unlike that of their Christian brethren. There is also a great sense of pride in being recognized as a person who has the ability to make a large gift. I spoke to Annabelle Fishman about someone who was clearly only one step away from bankruptcy. He owed everyone in town. But he increased his gift—a sizable one—to the Jewish Federation. Partly out of a sense of duty and, I suspect, mostly because he didn't want his friends to know how desperate his financial situation was.

The Jewish community is often criticized—usually by non-Jews—because their giving is limited to a great extent to Jewish programs and projects. And to those, they often give with a passion and a commitment which knows no limit. To their Federation, the Jewish Community Center, their temples and synagogues, the YMHA, and of course, to Israel. Over and over again to Israel. But of course! They give with boundless commitment to their own causes. Remember, people give to where there is the greatest emotional appeal and where they feel there is the most consequential opportunity for them to share. And dollars follow commitment.

One thing more about Jewish giving which tends to tie philanthropy to a strong sense of religious and community responsibility. Annabelle and Bernard Fishman really believe in giving. The family has done exceedingly well and their philantrophy has risen in direct propor-

tion to their income. The Fishmans feel strongly that
their friends should give, also. Annabelle Fishman says:
"We feel passionately about our Jewish charities, and
we expect our friends to feel the same as we do. You
know, if they are not givers, I find it really very hard to
understand and I don't see how they can really be friends
of ours. Little by little, people like that don't get invited
to our home or parties. It isn't so much that they aren't
givers, it's just that we tend to invite only friends—and
our friends are givers." Mrs. Fishman pointed out that
in communities where the Jewish population is very
strong, there is tremendous pressure on philanthropy,
but particularly to Jewish philanthropy. In Cleveland,
for instance, wealthy Jews are often ostracized if they do
not give heavily to the Jewish community. There is no
escaping. In every community, Jewish giving is docu-
mented and publicized, for everyone to see.

For the large donors to take pride. And for those who
don't give in proportion, to somehow find their own
niche outside the Jewish community.

Westmoreland Country Club is one of Pittsburgh's
most beautiful and expensive country clubs, one of the
finest in the nation. Its membership is Jewish. In a recent Wall Street Journal article it was reported that: "If
a non-giver wants to join, someone will mention, in a
nice way of course, that behaving responsibly means
remembering Jewish philanthropies. An influential law-
yer active in several charities favors tougher methods,
including ostracism, if friendly persuasion doesn't work.
'I wouldn't walk across the street to shake the hand of
someone who won't give.' "

There is a Yiddish expression: "Mir ken nischt erem

varen fun gaben tsadaka.'' You can never become poor by doing good deeds. The Jews really believe this and live it. They feel that philanthrophy is a wheel that keeps turning. The more that you give away, the more that comes back to you. Bunyan said: ''A man there was, and they called him mad; the more he gave, the more he had.'' Henry Ward Beecher really believed in this thesis. He reported that no one ever did anything worth doing who did not receive more in return than he gave.

* * * * *

James H. R. Cromwell is the son of one of the great benefactors of a prior era. He feels that people today will not talk about the duties and responsibilities that go with money. No one talks about uplifting the poor and sick, about the need to bring culture to the masses. These concerns are just not taken seriously. Today, anyone who talks that way is laughed at. He feels that in his mother's era, women had integrity, believed in what they were trying to do, believed it was important, believed it was virtually a holy obligation that went with wealth. But Cromwell says that those with that kind of a sense of responsibility are a vanishing breed. Even ''charity'' has become a dirty word. Not too long ago, to refer to someone as ''a patron of the arts'' was considered high and worthy praise. Today, it is a pejorative term.

Louise M. Davies feels clearly that giving is an obligation. She says that it is her duty and responsibility. ''I feel that everyone should give. It is the responsibility of anyone who has the money. The idea of giving is as old as man himself. We are born with the spark. I remember when I was a Girl Scout, we had to make a fire by rubbing two sticks together—and then we blew and blew, coaxing the spark to flame. We're all born with a spark, it just takes a little coaxing to get the flame.''

Clearly, the mega givers are not motivated by dire need, but rather are captivated by the opportunity, the challenge, the magic of being able to do something special, something others may not be in the position to do. Just as clearly, there is the strong sense of duty. Often, they feel they have been blessed with money— not always of their making—and they have a responsibility to use it and to give it away wisely. Duty, responsibility, stewardship.

Cyril Magnin says, "Great wealth carries great responsibility, a duty. I don't have as much as others, but what I do have I give way. I enjoy doing it. I give because it is something I want to do or perhaps it is something I feel I have to do. I'm not certain about that—the desire and the need get a bit mixed up. I feel it is a way of paying my debt. I've received so very much, so very much, and this is a way of helping pay it back.'' There was a long pause. Minutes. Then Magnin looked at me, eyes moist, he spoke slowly, carefully: "I have been very fortunate in my life. Ultra-lucky. I feel that everyone should give back a good portion of what they receive. I have gotten so much in life that I feel it is my responsibility to give it back.''

Some seem to have been born with the instinct and the need. Leo Roon is in his nineties, sparkling and vital. He was an extremely successful businessman and entrepreneur. He continues to be successful as a loving, help-

ful human being. He told me about how he was raised by an uncle. There was money in the family, but not a great deal of it. Leo won a small cash prize for excellence when he graduated from high school. He kept none of it for himself but shared it with his uncle and a few friends. "Even when I just started in business, and at that time things weren't going at all that well, my little company used to donate to the full limit allowed under the law. It was just something I wanted to do and expected that any good citizen would wish to do." In recent years, Leo Roon has given away over $10 million.

Virginia Piper was given the responsibility for continuing her husband's philanthropy. It was a great deal of money and Virginia Piper was determined to continue her husband's good work but to do it in her own way and for those organizations in which she was the most interested. "I learned a lot from my husband's giving. He felt that what he had on earth had been entrusted to him, and that the wealth that he had came from the grace of God. He felt strongly that he had a responsibility to share that gift from God. I feel the same way, that I have been put here to use the money I have available for the best work that I can.'

Robert Saligman says that ". . . Giving is sharing. Giving is absolutely essential to my life. Giving is like living, a day-to-day function. It is something I have to do." Leo Roon feels much the same way. He considers his philanthropy a personal matter, an individual responsibility and duty. "To me, giving is my life. It is something I must do. It is my way of paying back a debt I feel I owe."

Leo Beranek says that he has always had a history of

giving, from his earliest days. "It is a habit I formed early and as my income grew, I gave more. I think that giving is a habit. I feel an obligation to support organizations. I always have. I feel that people in my position ought to help society. If we don't, who will? I feel that when I make a gift, I am paying back to society what I owe it. It's quite common for a donor to want to repay the educational institution which gave him an important start. Similarly, a grateful patient feels a particular obligation to help the hospital which brought him back to health. There is a great personal drive and motivation in giving. It's partly duty and responsibility. But there are plenty of places to give. So much depends on what has a particular interest to you."

Givers feel the duty and the responsibility. The great need to pay back. What they find most difficult to understand is why others don't feel the same compulsion. Alex Spanos says: "There are a lot of people who don't know how to give and I feel sorry for them. They just don't understand how good they will feel when they do something for others." Leo Roon shares the same feeling of disappointment. "I just don't understand it. If they could only experience the wonderful feeling of sharing with others."

George Pardee says, "I really don't understand and can't explain why some people don't feel the same need or the responsibility to give. When Washington was paying seventy cents for every dollar I gave, I used to say to my friends: 'It's only costing you thirty cents to make a gift.' And they would tell me that that's thirty cents they don't want to spend!"

The answer now becomes better defined. There is

clear evidence that those who give do so out of a sense of duty and responsibility. For some, they seem to have been born with the commitment. For others, the need to share grows in proportion to their own financial growth.

*   *   *   *   *

Common to all the major donors is their compulsion to pass on to their families the same sense of responsibility. Leo Roon says: "I believe I've been able to pass on to my son the strong feeling I have for giving. He has established some very special programs through his generosity. The apple doesn't fall far from the tree. I am certain that parents are able to instill in their children the responsibility and joy of giving. It becomes a way of life. I know that in my own case, there was never any special incident that motivated me to give. The seed was always there. I am certain that while we did not talk a lot about it in our home, there was a great influence. I have always wanted to give and to serve. I remember when I graduated from high school and was given a $100 award for scholarship. I couldn't wait to give it away, I was so grateful. I guess I've always felt that way although as a youngster I didn't have much of anything to give."

Her mother was the great influence on Louise M. Davies. "Mother was always helping someone. We didn't have a lot of money or a lot of goods, but whatever there was she wanted to share it. I can still remember her saying, 'Hitch up the horse, we've got work to do.' And we'd be off and running to help a neighbor. I feel I learned a lot about giving through the generosity of my mother. I learned an awful lot. And she set a wonderful example. I've tried as much as possible to pass on to my children the importance of giving. They know how strongly I feel about it and I've shown them in a lot of different ways how important it is. I have tried to set a proper example and I can't do much more than that.''

James M. Gamble is the grandson of the founder of the Procter & Gamble Company, one of the country's leading suppliers of consumer goods. James Gamble says: "I am a giver because of my upbringing. There can be no question about it. My father taught me that being a good steward of our money was of the greatest importance. He used to say that we owe a great responsibility to society, a debt that we must repay. He used to say that we had nothing to do with the money we have and that it was given to us to repay society. I have that same strong commitment myself. There is a tradition in my family that started with my father, and I have tried to pass it on. The family believes in giving. We believe that money was provided to us to pass on to others.''

Gamble says that his dad was a tither. "Actually, he was more than a tither. He was deeply interested in the church and related organizations. I think that all of us in the family caught the special interest, also. I remember when I was a teenager and Dad would sit down with me to talk about my D.B.'s—Deductible Benevolences. Now, we did not have a large allowance. Dad didn't want to spoil us. But we always had the feeling that we had the responsibility to use a certain percentage of whatever allowance there was for important causes. Dad would talk with us about this and help us in our thinking. This made a great impression on me. I do the same thing with my children today.''

Alex Spanos has taught his children to give. "My children give. I've taught them that it's important. It's also one of the ways they can say thanks to me. They know that when they make a gift to a program that's important to me, that makes me extremely happy. Sometimes, if they want to give me a present or a gift, they know that the thing I like best or the thing that means the most to me, would be a gift to a favorite charity of mine. What else would they give me? A tie? A book? Last year, I had a benefit for some of my hospitals. One of my kids put in $20,000, and another $25,000. I can't tell you how happy that made me. My dad knew nothing about giving. It wasn't his fault, we just had nothing. We were lucky to have enough to eat. I think when you come from nothing, you know what it is like to be poor. You understand better what great joy it is to do something for others. If I feel that I can make others happy, if I feel that I can do good for others, it is of great satisfaction to me. I tried to help my children understand this feeling."

Dorothy Simmerly comes from a family of tremendous financial resources. At one time, one of the wealthiest families in the country. She says that she was surrounded by giving and felt the responsibility from the very beginning. "Mother was a giver and a very generous one. But she didn't talk to us directly about the importance of philanthropy. She didn't have to. The example she set was far more important than any words."

Marianne Mori agrees that children tend to learn by example. "I know that I encourage my children to give. They may not do as much I think is proper right now, but I know that the seed is properly planted. My father did not make a big thing out of giving. I guess I knew that he gave money here and there, but there was nothing named after him or anything like that. But I know that as far as I'm concerned, from as early as I can remember, I gave. When I was just a little girl, I always gave something to charity out of my small allowance. It was something I felt I just had to do.''

Four among those I interviewed came from families that were poor and where philanthropy was hardly a way of family life. "I've tried to instill in my children the importance of giving," says Cyril Magnin. "I don't feel that I've talked a great deal about it but I hope that they learn by my example. My parents didn't have the ability to give, there just wasn't any money. So we never talked about it as I grew up. But as I began earning money, I felt it was my obligation to do something. The Lord has been very good to me. I feel that there is much that I must return."

Arthur Rubloff says there was never any influence from his family or his father regarding giving. They never talked about it or about money. There was not much of it around. He feels, however, that for some reason from the very beginning, as soon as he started earning money, he was compelled to do something about giving. Robert Saligman's story is about the same. He told me that there was never any attempt to teach the concept of giving. "My family was so poor we didn't have any money to give. But it goes back years ago and I found that as soon as I was able to help others, I really enjoyed giving. I think it is terribly important to expose your children as much as possible to the tradition of giving."

The three Pardee brothers have had extraordinary success as land developers. And each is an extraordinary giver. Each has been identified with important causes and consequential programs. George Pardee says: "My mother and father were not givers. As a matter of fact, they went bankrupt during the Depression. I don't know what really has been the influence on me. I know that a lot of my friends don't share the same concern for philanthropy, and I can't understand it. My two brothers and I have done very well and each of us feels a strong commitment to giving. It is possible that I feel it is my way of giving back and showing thanks."

5
FIND A WAY TO RECOGNIZE

*"Under carefully controlled conditions,
organisms behave as they damn well please."*
—The Harvard Law of Animal Behavior

ROBERT CUNNINGHAM is one of the most prolific writers in the health field and considered one of the significant spokesmen for the healthcare delivery system in this nation. A former magazine publisher and editor at McGraw-Hill and a regular contributor to important journals, he tells of a Washington newsman who described philanthropy as people getting credit for giving back what their ancestors should never have taken in the first place. Witty, but it does not truly follow the pattern of today's large donor.

The key factor in giving possibly may be emotional.

And the emotion can be motivated by several factors. I am convinced that people do not give for tax reasons, although if there is an advantage, that is helpful. I am convinced they do not give logically. Passion, rather than reason, rules. Not many people make a list of half a dozen institutions that are asking them for gifts and then logically weigh the pros and cons of each institution. For most people, it is not cerebral. Some of those I interviewed characterized it as being close to a love affair. It is emotional. I love this place and I love what they are trying to do. It's exciting, and it appeals to me.

* * * * *

A careful review of those who have given a million dollars in the past four years indicates that the gift was made only after being directly asked to do so. This may be thought as being unduly basic, for one of the fundamental verities is that you must ask. It is one of the glaring truths of fund raising that a cause will be hurt more by those who would have said yes but were not asked, than by those who say no.

James N. Gamble is a professional's dream of what every volunteer should be like. The grandson of the founder of Proctor & Gamble, when Jim Gamble gets involved in a program he brings his total dedication and commitment. I remember when we were ready to launch a campaign for a woman's college in California, he told us that he couldn't take on any leadership for the project for a year. He was too heavily committed. We waited the year. It was worth it. He became totally immersed. His devotion to the program was contagious and it was suc-

cessful. It was precisely the same dedication which won the campaign for a hospital project where he and his family vacationed in Michigan. And he backs up every volunteer responsibility with zealous dollar support.

James Gamble says that he feels that there is a great deal of giving by association. People enjoy being a part of the club. People enjoy being associated with prominent men and women who are giving to the same cause. My interviewing bears this out. Very few enjoy the independent route, giving to an unpopular cause, giving to a highly experimental project. They much prefer the more accepted organization.

Individuals tend to follow a more conventional course. Foundations, on the other hand—especially those with a national orientation and a large staff—tend to look for experimental programs to support—especially those where there is a fire escape. Programs and projects they can give to for two or three years, and then phase out.

Individuals are likely to become most nonconforming in their bequests, not in their gifts while living. At the turn of the century, John Chaloner, a descendant of John Jacob Astor, established a foundation to help Americans study art abroad. Seven years later he was committed to a New York lunatic asylum. Ater three years, he escaped and fled to Philadelphia where he was pronounced sane. Some would say, well, that's Philadelphia for you. After brooding about the matter for twelve years, he amended the charter of his foundation to include three new purposes: to crusade against antiquated lunacy laws, to publish satirical poetry in Shakespearean sonnet form, and to keep his fortune from ever benefiting his brothers.

There are times when it is more difficult to identify the chief motivating factor. No single person probably has done more to provide financial support for health-care institutions than James Buchanan Duke, founder and benefactor of the Duke Endowment. His giving may not have been totally altruistic: "People ought to be healthy. If they ain't healthy, they can't work, and if they don't work, they ain't healthy, and if they can't work there ain't no profit in them."

Most large givers see the great visions, the bold dreams. They may see in their gift an opportunity to make the really significant difference in the world. To change mankind. To uncover a new answer for a dreaded disease. "In giving, I try to multiply myself," says W. Clement Stone. "I want to change the world and if the institution I'm giving to helps in my objective, then I am multiplying myself in making a gift."

Homer Watkins asked that he not be identified. He is the scion of a huge retail chain, a serious, intense man who is a careful and thoughtful donor. He and his family give $1 million gifts regularly to a variety of organizations, mostly local. Watkins says: "I want my gift to count for something. I want to know that what I do can possibly change the lives of thousands and hundreds of thousands. I want to know that because of my gift, I have made a difference. I have done something that no one else could have done."

The million dollar givers are selective, and there is virtually no evidence that they make a gift in that range without any prior experience of giving or history in the institution itself. The reverse is almost always the case and could justifiably be characterized as one of the major axioms of fund raising: those who give to you, those who will be making the largest gifts, those who are the most likely to be making a gift in the range of a million dollars, are those who have given to you in the past. So valid is this rule, you can actually take it to the bank! Your best and largest donors are those who have given to you in the past.

Giving is a habit. Very seldom does someone make a significantly large gift to an organization without the prior experience of giving to that institution. And almost never will that large gift be his last, but will almost certainly be followed by many others—often of increased size.

$$* \quad * \quad * \quad * \quad *$$

Cicero wrote two thousand years ago: "In nothing do men more nearly approach the gods than in doing good to their fellow men." This should be gratification enough, though without question recognition does play an important part for the donor. Louise M. Davies says that people like to be recognized. Take that as a given. "No matter what they say, they like the recognition. I don't need it and I don't seek it—but in a way I like it very much."

History has recorded few truly anonymous gifts. Most benefactors, who pretend to be anonymous, hide after conferring a gift, like Virgil's Galatea. She fled, but only after first making very certain that she had been seen by everyone.

The evidence supporting the importance of recognition is substantial. A condition of J. B. Duke's support for Trinity College at Durham was that it change its name to Duke University. Prior to that time, it was a small, Methodist school. The buildings of Harvard alone include the Widener Library, Houghton Library, Loeb Theatre, Harkness Commons, Kresge Hall, and Strauss Hall. Woebegotten is the campus or the medical center that doesn't have at least a dozen buildings, wings, pavilions, and libraries named after benefactors. Proof positive they have not been successful in the past in luring important dollars to their programs. There is another giveaway. The campus where buildings are named after past presidents and former deans. Ah, the beloved dean —but this almost always means that there wasn't a large donor who came forward.

It is extremely difficult to distinguish the line between those who wish recognition and those who really do not. I believe it is much wiser to err on the side of giving the recognition. Careful, thoughtful, considered recognition. Done with a quiet flair, a certain style. But recognition.

On the basis of my interviews, I am convinced that even though most of the million dollar givers did not expect a cannon-shot display of media and plaques, it meant a great deal to them to have others know what they had done. Dr Lawrence C. Kolp feels that what most people want is simply "to be sought." Dr. Kolp is one-time director of the New York State Institute of Psychiatry and chairman of the Psychology Department at Columbia University. He says that people want to be needed, want people to care about them, want people to listen to what they have to say. And want others to know about their good deeds.

Cyril Magnin is considered the godfather of all cul-

tural activities and the leader of all social events in the San Francisco Bay Area. Bright and vital in his mideighties, he is "Mr. San Francisco," the city's protocol chief and official greeter, and one of the greatest supporters of her arts. Singlehandedly, he built the Joseph Magnin Store, a dull carbon-copy of I. Magnin, into an empire of thirty-two stores. He's done it all. Official greeter of Presidents, a cameo role in an Academy Award film. A penthouse apartment on top of Nob Hill in the Mark Hopkins Hotel. A patron of the arts. At one time or another, on every major board on the area. The list goes on. His gift to a local museum made possible an important wing. When Tony Bennett played recently in the Venetian Room of the Fairmont Hotel, he stopped his song, asked that the spotlight be turned to a table close to the small stage. "Ladies and gentlemen, let me introduce Mr. San Francisco—Cyril Magnin. Your city is great, and he's the reason why."

Mr. Magnin's gifts to culture and the arts are substantial and regular. His largest gift houses a priceless jade collection in the Asian Art Wing of the M. H. deYoung Museum in San Francisco. It is named in honor of his parents and his late wife, the only memorial which carries the Magnin name. "The recognition of a gift means absolutely nothing to me, it makes no difference at all," says Magnin. "I do not give for the sake of getting my name in the paper or for personal aggrandizement. There is a personal satisfaction that I receive and that is simple enough. The Magnin Jade Room was really a major effort of mine and I wanted to do something to recognize my parents and my wife." The casual observer would note, however, that Magnin's name never fails to appear where he has been a patron of the symphony, the ballet, the arts, a membership in the museum, and so forth. But all done with very good taste.

It is her vitality, that's what you notice first of all about Louise M. Davies. Now in her eighties and enjoying life to its fullest, she is the widow of the founder of the American Presidents Lines. Her philanthropy makes her glow, it is the main stay of her life.

Mrs. Davies mentioned a fascinating aspect to one gift, the largest that has been given in the Bay Area to any program or organization. She disclaims the importance of recognition. "If I get it, I accept it; but I feel that's kind of the cream on top of the milk. The greatest recognition I get is the glow inside, and the sheer joy. When I gave my gift to the Center for the Performing Arts, I didn't want it named for me. It took me a great deal longer to decide to do that than it did to make the gift itself. I was convinced by others, however, that it would be the right thing to do for the good of the campaign. There was a feeling that people would follow my lead, and I think to some extent they did. I'm really happy now that is has worked out the way it did. It has been rather special for me. But at no time when I made the gift did I do it with the thought in mind that I would have something named for me."

Recognition and appreciation are closely linked. The donor, hand held high in protest, may deny any inclination for special recognition. But when one of the country's major zoos somehow managed to forget to invite its largest benefactor to an opening of a new section in the zoo—an addition the benefactor made possible—the zoo sealed its future for further gifts.

Mary G. Roebling is the chairman of the board of the New Jersey Trust Company in Newark. For years she has been one of the leading bankers in the country. Many years before, when she was the chief executive officer of the Trenton Trust Company, she taught me a valuable lesson. She was on the board of our college in Princeton, New Jersey, and was heading a special campaign. We were talking about strategy and the mechanics of the campaign and she said: "Now, Jerry, one thing you must remember. People like to be thanked, they want to know that what they have done is appreciated, really appreciated. When we get a gift that we think is special, let's find a way to thank the person at least seven times before we ever ask them again for another gift." Seven times! It seemed an almost impossible task. But if you plan for it, it can be done. The dividends are extraordinary.

We followed this "seven times" admonishment. There was a letter from the president. A letter from the chairman of the board. A handwritten note from the vice president. And a letter from the treasurer with the official receipt. Several months later, a note from a student who had received some scholarship assistance. A letter from the head of the department whose discipline had been particularly affected by the special campaign. A very brief personal note attached to the announcement of the groundbreaking ceremony, reminding the donor of how important their gift had been in making this day possible. Count them, seven times, and it was easy.

When the next campaign was announced, these people averaged gifts three times the amount of their original donation. Mary Roebling's suggestion was a valuable lesson. If I could guarantee you a continuing gift, not of the same amount, not double the amount, but three times the amount—wouldn't you work, work creatively, to plan for seven opportunities to show appreciation? Do it! Guarantees in fund raising are somewhat like a dog walking on hind legs. You may not understand exactly how it works, but you are amazed it can be done at all. This "Rule of Sevens" really works.

There is no end to the amount of opportunities you can seek to show appreciation. Robert M. Cunningham Jr. (*Asking and Giving: A Report on Hospital Philanthropy*, American Hospital Association, 1980) tells the story of Abram Sacher, the first chancellor of Brandeis University. He was considered to be without parallel in attracting support for his institution. Read on, this is surely one of the great stories of fund raising. "Dr. Sacher had attended a performance at the Brandeis theatre, which had been the gift of a generous donor, five or ten years after the gift was given, and then he had just dropped a handwritten note to the donor, taking no more than a minute to write a very personal message which went something like this: 'I just attended a performance of Hamlet in your theatre. I wanted you to know that the theatre was packed. The pleasure your theatre brought to the campus community was enormous and I want to thank you again.' Well, Dr. Sacher was wise enough to know that there was something prospectively good about that letter but he was also wise enough to know that this is part of the web of human society that ought to be fun to do. He did it, and he got a million dollars by return mail."

". . . And I want to thank you again. Without your

gift, the theatre would have been impossible.'' Now, Sacher was a great fund raiser and whether there was any ulterior motive other than simply expressing gratefulness, I leave to the reader.

The mind and persuasion of the fund raiser is devious and complex. He did receive a million dollar gift by return mail. There are not always those kinds of substantial rewards, but it is of very special significance to thank a person again, even long after protocol demands it. The original note of appreciation and accompanying receipt is expected. It is the unusual manner that you find to say ''thank you'' that is most remembered.

Man transcends death by finding meaning in life. To count for something. To make life meaningful. To serve mankind. To provide life and renewal from one generation to the next. This is the drive and desire among those who give. The giving itself appears to be reason sufficient. Acclaim and recognition to most are secondary, but important.

James Gamble says that the personal aggrandizement is not significant to him. ''I know that a lot of people do like their names on a wall but as far as I'm concerned, I don't feel that recognition is necessary to me. I know that it seems to be for others. As far as I'm concerned, I like to have the proper acknowledgement.''

Virginia Piper would like more than just acknowledgement. More than just the initial recognition. ''I like to have some follow-up. I want to be kept informed and updated. I like to keep posted on what's happening at the institution and particularly with the program that I've been involved with. The whole matter of being thanked is important to any donor. I think it's impressive when an organization demonstrates its appreciation in an appropriate way. Most of all, I want to be kept informed." When you review Mrs. Piper's record of giving, you notice that the major gifts that are repeated go to those institutions where her initial enthusiasm has been maintained. And where she has been kept informed!

Dorothy Simmerly's comment raises an interesting point. "I don't want any recognition. Actually for me, this is a minus. I find it embarrassing. The fact that I give is no credit to me. It doesn't take any great intellect. It takes money." Dmitri George put it another way: "What did it take for me to make my $1 million gift to the hospital? Well, first of all, it took the money to give it."

W. Clement Stone talks about a universal law, one which states that when you give without thought of return, you get it back a thousand times. He really believes that this is true, and he believes that this is particularly true in his case.

Stone told me that he recently gave a gift to a medical center in Korea. It was $1.5 million. It was in honor of a man, the memory of a man who means a great deal to Stone. "They wanted to name the building after me. I told them that I didn't want that, that's not what I had in mind. I gave the gift because of the vision of the priest who was so involved in the program. Name it after him. That's what I call being part of a great man's work. It would bother me personally if I gave only for the recognition. Flattery means nothing to me. I am a salesman. I can tell when it's being used on me, and I don't like it."

Stone shakes his head. "Recognition is not important to me. I give for the sake of giving." Just then, his secretary walked into the office as Stone continued. "I'm not after honors. You do good for the sake of doing good. I am not asking for recognition. I make a gift because I want to do it. I used to get quite upset about all of the fuss of recognition until I had one very wise man tell me: 'You know, Clem, you are very gracious in making your gifts. It's wonderful to be gracious in receiving recognition.' So if the recognition comes, I accept it. But I never seek it. In fact, sometimes I don't even get my gifts acknowledged."

I asked his secretary if it could possibly be true that there are times that his gift is not recognized. "It is indeed true. And those organizations do not get a second gift." And then I took her aside and asked if it was really true that Mr. Stone did not seek recognition. I have known him for years and no one would describe him as the shrinking violet type. He is outgoing, dynamic, and attuned to the media. "If he receives proper recognition, he accepts it. If he doesn't get it, I honestly don't think it bothers him."

Arthur Rubloff says that he does not look for memorials, but that he does not refuse recognition, either. If the organization wishes to show appreciation in a thoughtful and appropriate way, Rubloff accepts it. George Pardee says: "I think that the recognition of a gift and how its handled is important, especially at high levels. It needs to be handled with a sense of care and style, but the recognition is important. I don't believe in publicity. We don't give for recognition. I think that's something that has to be handled very carefully. We don't really look for it, but I must admit it's nice when people know what you've done."

It would be the unusual person who does not appreciate some special recognition, in one form or another. "But," says Leo Roon, "I want it to be used with discretion. Keep in mind that sometimes recognition of an individual is actually of great help to the institution. It encourages others and it can be a very effective and tasteful way of saying: 'See, we have a person who has done something special for us. Why don't you?' But I don't strive for recognition. I don't look for it. If it comes, I accept it with humility and, I believe, a certain amount of grace. Even without the recognition, I really get more pleasure out of my gifts than I probably deserve."

Community recognition is important to Marianne Mori. She feels that it is to everyone if they would admit it. "I give for five major reasons and I'm not certain that they are always in this order of importance: use, fame, love, political change, emotional. There's certainly ego involved and it really is present. I would like to gain some fame with my gift. That doesn't necessarily mean that I require tremendous recognition, but fame is different. That is of more lasting value. I want to know that my gift is really going for something that is significant."

Alex Spanos jumped from his chair. It was the question in the interview which evoked the most heated response. "I'll be honest with you. The impact of the gift, the recognition of the gift, is terribly important to me. I'm not certain I would make a gift unless I felt there was some recognition and a good deal of appreciation for it. I think if a person is really honest, I mean really honest, everyone would admit that this is important.

There isn't a man alive who doesn't give because of the recognition. I just don't believe it's possible.''

Among the million-dollar givers who were interviewed not one indicated that the gift was made solely to have their name memoralized. Amon Carter, Jr. said: ''Having our name attached to a building is not important to us. That's not what prompts the gift.'' Having worked with Amon Carter, I feel that that is his true feeling. However, several important buildings, a museum, and a magnificent architectural fountain in downtown Fort Worth are named after the family. A couplet from Pope's *Moral Essays* rings out:

> Who builds a Church to God and not to fame
> Will never mark the marble with his name.

My experience is that the donor, most often, does not want to ask for recognition but is grateful indeed for the suggestion. From a fund raising standpoint, that type of giving begets additional giving. From the donor and from others.

The smart fund raiser works with the donor in planning for the recognition. And keeps the donor informed on a regular basis of the progress. If it is a construction program, for instance, the opportunities are unlimited. Dmitri George reported that after his gift was made, there seemed to be no end to the processional from the hospital: ''The architects visited me to show me their plans and ask me my reaction. The administrator called on me regularly to keep me informed of the progress of the construction. The director of development wrote me letters and sent me clippings. The groundbreaking was a three-ring circus. I never felt as appreciated. I didn't seek the recognition but it turned out that it meant a great deal to me." Guess where Mr. George will make his next major gift?

In expressing appreciation, I propose that the best general rule to follow is that you can never do enough. In giving recognition, do everything and anything that is within proper taste and appropriate to the donor.

It is a modern Damon and Pythias story. Bill passes John on the street. There's absolutely no recognition from John. Bill catches up with him, stops him, twists him around. "John, how can you pass me on the street like that, without even a word of recognition? Eight or ten years ago, when you were out of work, my wife and I took you into our home and you lived with us for two years. You slept on our bed and you ate our food, and we never charged you anything. I helped you find your first big job, and I personally paid for the suit of clothes and the shoes that you wore to that interview. I introduced you to the girl that you married eight years ago and I gave you the money for your honeymoon. I paid for your first car and when your kid was sick, I paid for most of the hospital bill. How can you pass me on the street like this without even a hello?" John turned and walked away. "But what have you done for me lately?"

The organization must make the opportunity to show appreciation, even if the donor has not done anything lately for the organization, and the rule of "seven times" is an invaluable one. The proper recognition and appreciation ensures continued giving.

6
YOU WIN WITH BOLD PLANS

"Hark! Hark! The dogs do bark.
The beggars are coming to town;
Some in rags, some in tags,
Some in velvet gowns.
—Mother Goose

YOU HAVE HEARD about selling the sizzle. Big and bold programs sell. The exciting programs. Innovative twists, tantalizing packaging. Some campaigns are moribund because they are lackluster, ho-hum carbon copies of other projects. We have conducted feasibility tests on some campaigns that show a lack of either the necessary leadership or dollars to get the campaign started. Then— by a careful addition, by injecting a new dimension, by expanding the parameters—we were able to develop a winning package. In some cases, it actually meant adding millions of dollars to the final objective. It also meant adding the sizzle. W. Clement Stone says: "High achievers make big plans. Those are the kind of people and institutions I like to support."

Make no small plans. Donors want to cross over thresholds and be a part of expanding new horizons. Major donors want to soar to heights others have not reached, or cannot reach. They give to dreams and visions that glow.

But beware. An individual is much less likely to want to take on controversy. A big, bold plan; but not controversy. The individual mega givers tend to stay with the more conventional programs. Almost every instance of a large individual gift is for a conventional project. Foundations are in a better position to take on non-popular issues, even controversy. Often, in today's world, to be relevant is to risk controversy. Ford Foundation president McGeorge Bundy says: "A foundation should not shrink from important issues even if they become controversial, and we do not intend to back away from the hot issues."

Foundations are much more likely to wish to become involved in a program where they can offer funds to get a new program launched. But they seek an escape hatch, a way to get involved and out of the program in a few years. Individuals are much more likely to want a program they can continue to support.

Foundations are made up of people—men and women—who have in many respects the same emotional incentives and motivations for making a gift as individuals. But the major foundations, especially those with a national orientation and a large staff, tend to be much more clinical in their grant-giving. A bit more coldhearted and objective. One college fund raiser tells of the foundation executive he called on who had a glass eye. He could always tell which of the two eyes was the glass one—it was the more compassionate of the two.

Large donors enjoy giving seed money. They plant the seed by making a large gift. This in turn generates more funds and encourages a wider circle of activities. Large donors enjoy being the yeast, not the pablum. Major foundations prefer the pump-priming concept; or as one foundation executive described it: "We like to provide an extra engine to help the train up the slope. But we like to get out and the uncoupling can be painful." Major donors do not bounce back and forth, from one program and one organization to another. They tend to stay with those programs and activities which have been of interest to them over a long period. Old school ties can be very binding. The relationship with the Boy Scouts or the YMCA, very enduring. An association with a hospital can have great sentimental attachment. They do not give up these relationships easily. When a donor's giving pattern has been established over a long period, it is not often changed.

* * * * *

In every institution, strong financial support and a record of giving has to be present. And to meet today's and tomorrow's needs, on an ever-increasing scale. Balancing a budget, however, must not be done at the cost of independence or integrity of the institution. The mission of the organization remains supreme. In fact, it is by far the most salable commodity. The former president of Princeton, Harold Dodds, said: "A college or university must live dangerously or die on the vine." The same can be said of every organization. A vital, growing, dynamic institution must live no other way. If it does, it may not survive. Those which just tread water will sink in time. And no thoughtful donor wishes to help a sinking organization. Prospective donors, no matter how strong the sales presentation, will not give sacrificially to a campaign "To Save the Sinking Titantic."

The best prospects for a gift, a major gift, are those who have already given. Look here first for your best prospects. The more a person gives, the more likely he or she is to give more. And more. Giving begets giving. It is a habit. With only one exception among those I interviewed was there an individual who made a million dollar gift where the donation represented the first really sizable experience.

Often, in developing a prospect list for a campaign program, men and women with quite sizable financial resources are suggested. If they are not known donors, if they have not had the thrill and joy of giving in the past, chances are you will not be able to pry the big gift from them. But start, start now. Their smaller gift, one which will probably disappoint you, will be the beginning. With the proper kind of appreciation and recognition, you are certain to get more. Giving begets giving.

Why is it that the institution in the gravest danger, the one with the most critical need, does not necessarily capture the imagination of the major donor? It is because men and women enjoy giving to a program that is already popular. They enjoy the momentum of the bandwagon, giving to a program which has already received acceptance. No one wants to give to a losing cause. Few people are interested in a rescue mission. That is very likely why the more successful institutions, the wealthier ones, become more successful and wealthier. The poor, get poorer. Donors enjoy giving for exciting programs and leave it to others to come along later to pick up the dollar needs.

Donors do not give to critical needs. They give to bold and dramatic opportunities.

Big donors do not give recklessly or dangerously. By and large, they don't live their lives that way and they don't like giving their money in that manner. A potentially explosive project will most often not be of the greatest interest to them.

W. Clement Stone says that he is not interested in sharing in financial plights or deficit fights. He says that his whole life is dedicated to changing the lives of individuals, and you don't do that by bailing an institution out of poor financial management.

* * * * *

Giving to a specific project was not a major factor in securing the million dollar gift. First and foremost, the donor was interested in the organization itself. That was of primary concern. The specific project may have been tantalizing, challenging, or inventive. But it was the love for the organization that made the difference. First, sell the organization and its mission. Then talk about the specific project. Robert Saligman says: "The largest gift I have made to an organization was for a home for the elderly. It was the home itself that got me most interested, not a specific project. I feel that there is a great need among the elderly. I felt that this was something I had to do. George Pardee says that he very seldom designates his gifts for a specific project. "If I really believe in the organization, I feel the board and the staff are smart enough to use the money where it will do the most good." Amon Carter, Jr. agrees: "I gave my money to the YMCA because I really believe in the organization. A specific program doesn't interest me. The YMCA does."

It is quite clear. There is no such thing as a shortage of major donors. There is only a shortage of great ideas to raise money. A desperate need for vision and dreams.

* * * * *

Benjamin Franklin was this nation's first great fund raiser. He singlehandedly developed strategy, implemented the plans, and secured the funds for the Pennsylvania Hospital. It was Mr. Franklin who first conceived the idea for the "matching gift." While the concept may have appeal among smaller donors, it seems to have little effect with the million dollar givers. W. Clement Stone says: "I don't mind being a loner in my giving. I often give to organizations that no one knows I've given to. If my heart is in the program of the organization, that's what I give to." Leo Roon says that what others give to a program does have an influence on him but that a matching gift has little impact on what he does. "A matching gift has never affected the size of my own giving but it does encourage me to participate on some level."

Dorothy Simmerly says: "I feel sorry for those who don't give. But I hate counting other people's money. I think this is so unfair. And I don't like people deciding what I should give to. A matching gift has absolutely no effect on my giving. I think I may even have a negative reaction to it." Alex Spanos says that a matching gift has never encouraged him to make a sizable gift although he tends to participate if he knows that others are supporting the program heavily. He likes being part of something that is successful.

Corporations tend to give to community programs. A new building for the YMCA, a swimming pool for the YW, an alcohol treatment center for the Salvation Army, a camp for the Boy Scouts, a new wing for the hospital. This is their effective way of demonstrating corporate concern and responsibility. The large donor will often give to a community capital endeavor, but it will most likely be out of love for the particular organization than from a sense of civic pride or responsibility.

Amon Carter, Jr. says: ".There are many campaigns in Fort Worth and I give to most of them. But I give the largest amount of my money to the YMCA because I really believe in it." Homer Watkins reports that his four brothers have pretty much determined what their particular interests are in the city where they live. Each gives to all major causes but in the case of each, the bulk of their giving is directed to the organization of their special interest.

Leo Roon much prefers a more global view although he gives to most local causes. "What I am really interested in are projects which can provide a general good to all of mankind. A local hospital is important. I have supported many. But medical research is something special because giving to that can help unlock something that will be of good to all mankind.'' Arthur Rubloff says: ''I've given 45 years of my life to civic projects. I guess there's really nothing major in Chicago that has gone on that I haven't been involved in and given to.'' But his three major multi-million dollar gifts have all gone to programs with broader platform than merely a civic one.

Alex G. Spanos is a man of strong feelings and he has an opinion on just about everything. He is totally candid, sometimes brutally so. He fills a room with his laugh. He has given generously to his university, to his alma mater, the University of the Pacific. He is likely one of their most generous benefactors. He gives to countless other organizations and institutions. His office dress is informal, he sports a crew cut, and he is as trim as the day he graduated from college. He is the largest builder of apartments in the world and has amassed a fortune. He is considered to be one of the wealthiest Greeks in the United States. And there are many wealthy Greeks in this country.

Spanos spent his youth in near-poverty. A self-made man, a private person, simple tastes. He dotes on his family and says that his wife has been the greatest influence on his life. His other passion is golf. A scratch player. You wouldn't expect anything else from Alex Spanos. Everything he does, he does well.

Alex Spanos has given several million dollars to his alma mater. ''I don't know why really. But I believe in it. I really do believe in it. That's my most important charity. I went to school there and it also happens to be in my community. It means a lot to me. But there are a lot of other organizations in the city to which I don't give. I give to the university not out of any sense of civic responsibility; I give to it because it's my university.''

Dorothy Simmerly thought carefully. ''I really feel I have a responsibility to my community, and that doesn't only mean where I live. By 'community,' I am taking a much broader outlook—the area, the region, possibly the world. That's my community. I give to hospitals and schools and to things of that sort because I feel it is my responsibility. This has nothing to do with civic pride. It has to do with my sense of responsibility.''

Do the prestigious institutions gain support because of their national reputation and regard? I imagine this helps although it would not explain the million dollar gifts to lesser organizations. The Harvards, the Mayo Clinics, the Metropolitan Museums of Art—do they garner money because of their national reputation or because they merit support? Much more likely the latter, and evidence tends to support this.

Dorothy Simmerly graduated from one of the more prestigious colleges in the country. ''I gave to my school a few years after I graduated but I made it very clear to them that this would be the last gift they would ever receive from me and it was. They are so rich and they really don't need my money. I prefer giving to other things. Organizations that really need my help.'' Leo Roon has given $6 million to Scripps Clinic and Research Foundation. ''I didn't make my gift because of their national reputation, although that is considerable. I

really felt that by giving to Scripps there was an opportunity to make a difference to serve man. That is what I'm
really after. I give a great deal of money to organizations
that do not have a national platform.''

7
SEIZE THE MAGIC MOMENT

"Success is achieved by those who try and ask."
—W. Clement Stone

IT IS PROBABLY best that he remain nameless. I think he would prefer it that way. He is the popular minister of one of the nation's largest Methodist churches. Recently, at a small gathering of other ministers, he related this story.

A teachable moment. Each person around the table hung on every word. Our minister friend spoke with some emotion; he had just the day before learned one of the greatest lessons of fund raising. The memory was still vivid.

The wealthiest member of his congregation, a widow, was in the hospital. A long term illness was, sadly, moving at its slow pace to end her life. The minister made regular calls over a period of nearly three months, at least two times a week and often more than that. "Let's be honest, gentlemen," said the minister to the group. "I considered it my pastoral duty to visit with that faithful servant, one of the most active women in my congregation. I wasn't unmindful, however, that she was also of immense wealth and that because of her long years with our church, we were certain to be the beneficiary of her large estate. There were no children, no relatives, only her great, abiding love for our church. She often spoke to me, even before her illness, of all she hoped to do for the church.

"I visited her faithfully, week in and week out. I brought her spiritual encouragement, often small gifts like stationery, and held her hand while I prayed with her. It was a ministry of love. She was easily one of the most popular women in the congregation and one of my longtime favorites.

"Finally, after all of that suffering, the end came and she slipped quietly into the night. There would be no more suffering. That was about a month ago. Yesterday, I found out from her attorney—also a member of our congregation—about the disposition of her estate.

"While in the hospital, she had arranged her affairs. She left her entire estate to a Midwestern university, her husband's alma mater. I was incredulous and I must say, God help me, more than disappointed. What happened? I asked the attorney. It turned out that the priest who was the president of the University came by the hospital one day for a visit. He asked her for a gift. He asked her! That's all he did. He asked. It occurred to me that in all of the time I had known her and in all my visits, I never asked for a gift. I took that for granted.''

As you read this story, the moral is clearly recognizable, even to the uninitiated. But the rule is so often neglected and is one of the major stumbling blocks of the fund raiser. You must ask for the order!

Samuel Skaggs gave a million dollar donation to Iliff School of Theology. Earl Wood was director of development of the school, and was responsible for getting the gift. It was the largest donation the seminary had ever received. It was also the largest gift Mr. Skaggs had ever given to a United Methodist cause. Later, the inevitable question was asked. It went something like this: ''Mr. Skaggs, you have been a loyal member of the church for years and have been devoted to our work. You have given generously to other organizations. How does it happen that this is the very first time you have given this large a gift to a Methodist cause?'' Mr. Skaggs said, ''This is the first time anyone ever asked me.''

Earl Wood asked for the order.

Sending a letter or telephoning simply won't do. Not for the large gift. That's stating the obvious. No one ever got milk out of a cow by sending a letter. You get your stool right next to Betsy, stroke her properly, and keep working at it. That's how you get the large gift. Lots of stroking.

Stroking includes continuous and innovative cultivation. A steady, unending stream. You must find ways to keep your institution's name in front of the donor. One of Harold J. Seymour's most often quoted homilies is:

"You don't make a pickle by taking a cucumber and sprinkling a little vinegar over it. You immerse it!"

* * * * *

No question about it, the quintessence of successful fund raising is the careful and sometimes imaginative matching of askers to givers. Or, as one person so aptly put it, the hunter and the hunted. The question is, who is precisely the right person to do the hunting? From my observation, the old adage of peer-on-peer may not necessarily be the only answer. It indeed may not be an answer at all. Those who gave a million dollars were quite clear on the subject.

This question alone represents one of the greatest departures from what has been a sound and basic fund raising procedure I have been practicing myself for years. Just as in an old biblical story, retold with love seven times a hundred thousand, the long-cherished concept is that volunteers and peers do the soliciting and are the most effective solicitors. Not so. Not in every case. Every situation is an opportunity for a highly thought-out and considered plan. Like waging war, a separate campaign may be needed for each individual donor. Each situation is different.

Dr. Leo Beranek and his wife gave $1 million to the Boston Symphony Orchestra, the largest gift ever made to the one hundred year old organization. Beranek is a co-founder of a Cambridge acoustical engineering firm, chairman of Boston Broadcasters, Inc., and co-founder and former president of Boston TV channel 5. The gift was electrifying and surprising to the Boston community. Well, it even surprised Beranek a bit! It was the *largest gift he had made up to that time. He has since increased his generosity. But it was his gift which unlocked the horde of others and provided the success pattern for the symphony campaign.*

Beranek says, "I'm kind of resistant to all solicitors. It would be typical of me to know the organization pretty well before I make a gift. I don't need anyone coming in to make a sale. It's not a sales pitch that I need. As a matter of fact, I really don't like it. I would say that in many of the situations in which I give—probably two-thirds of all of my giving—no one makes an official call. I decide what I'm going to do. Once in a while a close friend will call on me and because of the friendship, I feel compelled to do something. But it's always a very small gift, a token, a couple hundred dollars."

Beranek's comment also lays to rest the question of a good friend making the call on a potential donor. He is almost certain to get something, but it will not be a gift of any magnitude unless the donor has great regard for the institution. Leo Roon says: "If a friend asks me for a gift and I'm not particularly interested in the organization, chances are that I'll do something, maybe a few thousand. But I certainly won't make a large gift to an organization I'm not particularly interested in, even if a friend calls."

"It doesn't matter who makes the call," says Cyril Magnin, "it could be almost anyone. It is the project which attracts me, which compels me. Not the person. I suppose I am impressed if someone important takes time to call on me for a gift. But it really doesn't make any difference. Even if a friend, a dear friend, calls on me, it wouldn't make any difference. I've learned to give only to programs which I feel are worthy and need help. Programs where my help can make a difference.'' James Gamble feels strongly that the president of an institution, the chief executive officer, should become heavily involved in the fund raising process. ''I like to have the president make the call and I like going with the president to make the call. He ought to be the person who is in the best position possible of interpreting the institution. If he can't, who can? The leverage of the solicitor doesn't count a bit if you don't have an interest in the institution. I don't care who makes the call or at what level. If I'm not interested in the organization, I'm not going to do anything. Oh, I might give a small amount just to buy them off, but that's it.''

He is eighty years old. Time has diminished his hearing, weakened his eyes, and slowed his gait—but not by much. And the years have not diminished his flamboyance and style one iota. Arthur Rubloff—a rags-to-riches man and a chronic giver. Some say that he owns most of downtown Chicago, and a suburb or two. That is, of course, an overstatement. But not by much. He is credited for naming and developing Chicago's Magnificent Mile, developing the North Loop area, and constructing Sandburg Village. He still actively heads one of the largest fully diversified real estate firms in the nation. Listed as one of the best dressed men in America, it is not uncommon to see him racing down Michigan Avenue, resplendent in his tailored suit, a bowler hat, and a gold topped cane.

Last year, Arthur Rubloff gave $5 million to both the University of Chicago and Northwestern University. ''It wasn't a case of any special loyalty to either institution

—they're both distinguished universities. In the case of the University of Chicago, I am providing the intensive care center for the hospital. At Northwestern, I am giving them their library which will be on the Lake and will also serve as the law library. I had no particular interest in either project—I gave because of my regard for both institutions. In the case of both universities, the president called on me and, I think for these two projects, that was the right person. I do not think I would have reacted as well to a volunteer. In the case of both presidents, they were most effective in asking for the gift." Rubloff, by the way, did not attend either university.

Father Hesburg, the distinguished president of Notre Dame University, is considered one of the finest fund raisers in the business. He brings a feeling of integrity and commitment to every call. Virginia Piper was impressed when he called on her. "It really doesn't matter who makes the call. I don't think that I would ever give to a total stranger, in fact I don't think I would be willing to see someone I didn't know. But I don't think it really matters who makes the call just so I have the feeling that it is a person of integrity and honesty. I remember when Father Hesburg called on me to make a gift to Notre Dame in memory of my husband. I knew Father Hesburg for some time and have always had a tremendous respect for him. I was flattered that he would make the call. But the project was just right. The thought of having something very special on the campus for Paul. I decided right away to go ahead but almost anyone could have made that call, and that doesn't take anything away from Father Hesburg whom I greatly admire. It was the right project and the right time."

Virginia Piper is attractive, has a bright sense of humor, and has a magnificently positive outlook on life. Her age is not really important. She is one of those fortunate ones who will never look or grow old. She lives in Arizona, surrounded by bright and vivid colors. They match her personality. In her home the flowers, the wallpaper, the furniture fabric are all a symphony of color. Her first husband was Paul Galvin, founder and the largest shareholder in the Motorola Company. It is mostly that inheritance that she has invested carefully and used wisely for a wide variety of organizational and church activities. There is a certain vulnerability about her. She has been hurt badly by several who have been the recipients of her generous support. That does not seem to have deterred her in any way from pursuing vigorously ways that she might help others.

Mrs. Piper says that it has to be just the right person who calls on her. "Overbearing people, egotistical people, bore me. It's a hard thing for me to want to do anything for them. They really turn me off. I enjoy the people I give to. It has been one of the great benefits of giving. The person who represents the institution really makes the difference for me. I must have faith in that person."

Dorothy Simmerly gave the largest gift to a recent national campaign for a major church group. The person who made the call, who got the gift, was the national head of the church, a man of the cloth. "It was the first time I'd met him. I was greatly impressed with his tremendous energy and vision. I think I was sold from the beginning and I must say, too, that I felt good about being called on by the highest man in the church. He called on me to talk about my gift to the program. He told me about the project and I found it to be exciting and I wanted to do something for the church. The whole thing was providential. It all fit together. I reacted in a positive way to the project immediately and I took a little time to think it over. My reactions were calculated —more like a man than a woman, I believe—I did think it through.''

Dorothy Simmerly is a person of conviction. ''I need to make up my own mind. I simply won't be pushed into anything. There's no way of embarrassing me or coercing me into something I don't want to be a part of. I don't care who makes a call on me. It can be a staff person or a board member. Now that I think about it, it is probably more effective if a staff member comes who can really give me the answers to all the questions I ask. And I ask plenty. I've thought about this before and I think it is a little less influential when a woman asks me for a large gift. I can't explain that but it doesn't have quite the impact.'' Mrs. Simmerly can be stubborn, too. ''I give most often without actually going through a sales presentation. I tend to choose the institutions I want to give to. Actually, it is very hard to make an appointment with me and I can't remember when I have actually talked with someone I did not know or care to talk with. It's not very easy to get by my secretary.''

These comments underline the importance of having the right person make the contact. It may be a volunteer, it may be a friend, or it may be staff. But the right person. That's the key. And then the approach. That's important. Firm, interpretive, persuasive. But any attempt at what appears to be heavyhandedness is a turn-off.

Paul Davies is a solid fund raiser. He says that he never pressed a designated amount on anyone. "I just put it before him and if his eyes don't light up right off, I pull it away and begin thinking about an alternative." One master fund raiser calls his method "playing for the flinch." He aims extremely high and if the donor doesn't flinch, he takes a different approach and aims even higher. He keeps increasing the level until the donor finally flinches. And then he stops. Another fund raiser calls his method "the white knuckle" approach. He tentatively uses a gift level, one higher than the next. When he notices that a donor is gripping his chair and his knuckles are turning white, he stops at that level. Kim Klein says that first "you imagine what success looks like. Talk about the amount you want, tell the donor why you want it, then repeat the amount. Then be quiet and wait for them to say 'yes'."

One college president claims that fund raising is the art of plucking the goose to obtain the largest amount of feathers, with the least possible amount of hissing.

The story is told of one volunteer fund raiser at a university who called on a prospect, an alumnus, for his gift to their major campaign. The interview was not going well at all. "I'm fed up and tired with what's going on. It's not the same old school today as it was when I went there. I'm angry with the students, their long hair, their easy habits, and I don't like the way the university is being run. Sometime ago, I decided to leave $500,000 in my will to the school. I'm so disgusted with the university now that I called my attorney the other day and told him to take the school out of my will.'' There was hardly a pause; the response was nonplussed: ''Why didn't you tell me it was a million dollar gift instead of $500,000? I would have been twice as upset and it wouldn't have cost you a penny more.''

Marianne Mori is another one who does not care who makes the call. ''People don't really influence me in my giving, no matter who comes to make the call. I like to hear a good, sound rationale regarding the project and its validity. I'll make up my own mind, no matter how persuasive the solicitor is. I don't like people who tell me what I must do or should do. I resist that kind of giving and it almost always turn me off. It can be a board member or a staff person who asks me for the gift, that part doesn't matter. If there's someone I don't know or respect, it is almost certain I would not see him in the first place.''

Sydney Smith is in total agreement with Mrs. Mori. Smith says that man is unquestionably a benevolent animal. ''A'' never sees ''B'' in dire distress without thinking that ''C'' ought to do something immediately to relieve him. Large donors resist the ''you must do this'' approach. Everyone does. It is not the way to raise major funds.

It is a plain fact of fund raising that it is often more difficult to get an appointment than it is to get the gift. The known philanthropist has been called on before, and you can count on that. He tends to be a cynic, faced with a never-ending pleading for gifts, and has been known to develop a hide the thickness of a rhinoceros'. Getting the interview can be the most important strategy of all. Making the appointment is perhaps the most effective use of the peer-on-peer theory. Get a peer or a friend to make the appointment. Have them go along on the call, along with a staff person. That could be a formidable combination.

Dortch Oldham is one of Nashville's most respected citizens. A leader, a doer, a giver. He was owner of the Southwestern Corp., a company that hires over one thousand college students to sell a variety of books door to door. Over the years, the company has provided students with many opportunities to earn money for tuition and school expenses. Dortch took advantage of this opportunity when he was a penniless college student.

Mr. Oldham has great regard for the president of his alma mater. That was an important element in his making a million dollar gift to the university. He says that no one can raise money like the chief staff person. It's a key factor.''

Louise M. Davies is not easily influenced. ''It really doesn't matter to me at all who makes the call for a gift. When I made my $5 million gift, the solicitor wasn't my closest friend or someone who has the most influence over me. I just thought that the project was the most important thing in the world. Sometimes I have very close friends who call on me for a gift. Then I feel obligated to do something because it's them, and not because of the program. But even at that, I would never give the closest of my friends anything over a few hundred dollars at the most for a program I really didn't care about. I just wouldn't be influenced that way. And I don't like to be told what to give. When somebody says, 'I think you ought to do this or that,' I just bristle, my back goes up. For me, that's about the worst thing a person could do, tell me what to give. I think it is terribly bad psychology.''

There is no one more dedicated than "a grateful patient." And in this case, there is surely no one more effective to make the call than the physician himself who took care of the patient. That could very well result in a large gift. Edmund L. Keeney, M.D., is the retired director of the Scripps Clinic and Research Foundation. He never asks for money but he is considered one of the most successful fund raisers in the business. When he visits with a prospect, he talks about a new medical library, he talks about a new cancer research center, he talks about a new surgical suite, and he talks and he talks. He always talks about ''something'' but he never talks about money. He sells the product, and he does it with such conviction and persuasiveness that it is hard to resist.

George Pardee tells how having ''the right'' person call on him can make the difference. ''I'm really interested in the Boy Scouts so when they called on me the first time for the YMCA capital program, I just wasn't quite as interested. That's no reflection on the Y—it's just that it isn't as dear to me as the Boy Scouts. The second time around, well, the person who made the call on me was the difference. I have so much respect for him, I felt that I had to do something. It wasn't nearly as much as I give to some of my other charities, but it wasn't insignificant, either. I like to be called on by the right person. No matter how worthy the cause, the solicitor has to be someone I respect. I think it's better to have the volunteer ask but I'm not sure that it matters a great deal and it really doesn't work all that much differently. It has to be someone who knows the program.''

"The right person" seems to work in the case of W. Clement Stone, also. "I like to have a person of influence call on me and I do understand the peer-on-peer concept. When [naming one of Chicago's leading industrialists] walks in the door and says 'Clem, I really need your help,' you can bet I always make a gift. The same is true when Bob Schuller calls. But the right staff member can do a good job, too. I like to see a staff person who'll make good, pragmatic common sense."

Respect seems to be the pivotal word in so many of these comments. Robert Saligman says: "I think it is extremely important who asks you to make the gift. It doesn't matter to me whether it is a staff person, a volunteer, or a friend—but it better be someone for whom I have respect. I think getting the right person to make the contact is the key to getting a gift at the right size. But for me, it can be anyone I respect." Alex Spanos says: "Of course it's important who makes the call. Below the level of president, the staff can't sell me anything. Most of the time I wouldn't give them the chance to see me. It's got to be the top person. I've got to tell you that I'm really impressed when the chairman of the board, a couple board members, and the president come into my office to see me. That's impressive. That means that I am important enough for them to take the time. When they sit down in the office like that, I'm ready to listen."

"I think it's important who makes the call," says Leo Roon. "He had better be someone I really respect. That means it can be a staff person or a board member—that doesn't really matter, just so I respect him. It doesn't necessarily have to be a peer, either, or someone who

will give or has given as much as I. But it better be
someone for whom I have regard.''

There was another thread which ran through most of
the interviews. Once again, it defied one of the old
rules. It has been said so often that it has become virtually the gospel—but I find that it is not necessarily true. It
has been said that two people can make an effective call
but that more than that can be overwhelming to a donor.
Not true! I find that it can be most persuasive and impressive to have three or four attend one of the early
sessions with a donor. Try it. A friend, the chief executive officer, the chairman of the campaign, and a person
who has made a gift at the level you seek from the prospective donor. You orchestrate the discussion carefully.
Very carefully. The prospective donor knows he's in for
a difficult time, but somehow he seems to enjoy the
fuss. He's impressed that so many important people
have taken the time to make the call. It must be important to them. It must be an important program. It must
be a gift at an important level they are seeking. Subsequent calls—and you had better prepare for additional
discussions for it is a major gift you are after—can be
handled by fewer, or by one person.

Another good rule to follow is that it is almost certain
that you will require several calls, sometimes many, to
get a gift at the level you are after.

I did not test this next matter but it is interesting to
note that of all the million dollar gifts which I reviewed,
only one presentation was made at lunch. There is no
scientific data to substantiate this, but a meal—with all
of the clang and clatter, table-hopping, and irrelevant
chatter—takes away measurably from the focus and ob-

jective of the meeting. A waiter asking for the dessert order at precisely the wrong time can cause an unnerving interruption. The magic moment is lost.

8
THE SPOUSE COUNTS

"Success is not searching for you. You must do the seeking. Destiny is not a matter of chance, it is a matter of choice; it is not a thing to be waited for, it is a thing to be achieved."
—William Jennings Bryan

WOMEN LIVE LONGER than men. This is a statistical fact. In fact, it is said that no one lives longer than a widow who has named your organization in her will.

We take so little advantage of this. During the life of the wealthy man who serves on your board, be certain that his wife is invited, as much as possible, to participate in programs and activities. Be sure she receives information, is called on. Create opportunities for the two of them to join in organizational events, annual meetings, retreats. When the man sits on the dais or is recognized for his leadership or a gift, give his wife equal attention. It is the right thing to do. And it will pay. And if the man precedes his wife, consider adding her to the board. His dedication to the organization will continue through her. And his benevolences.

Don't wait until you plan on asking for a gift before paying attention to the widow. It may be too late. Her attention and commitment may be diverted to another organization. Involve her in the program as soon as possible. It will pay eminently good results to your organization and, at the same time, help the widow through her bereavement.

In 1961, Frances Mason conducted a study which has relevance even today. Ms. Mason was trained in survey and public relations work. She studied the pattern of philanthropy of women who gave generously to voluntary agencies in their communities. There was no indication in the material of how many women were contacted and the impression is that it was focused only on local philanthropy. The survey consisted of depth interviews with prominent women, each a participant rather than a spectator in the affairs of the community. The survey was limited and makes no claim to scientific substantiation. Also, although the amount of their philanthropy was not indicated, it appears that it did not consist of major gifts in the range of a million dollars. Still, the study does describe certain factors that indicate a pattern in the giving habits of women.

Frances Mason discovered that any form of pressure was keenly resented by the women she studied and they reacted against it. Solicitors applying pressure usually receive an unequivocal nothing. Once the size of the major gifts and of the larger gifts was decided upon, the decision stood regardless of who beat upon the doors during the year. It was found, however, that smaller gifts were made when a persistent friend exerted influence.

Not surprisingly, the major beneficiaries of each woman interviewed remained the same for years, with the largest gift going to the organization which had won interest, participation, and loyalty early in their adult lives. Only rarely were new beneficiaries added to their philanthropy. One woman said: ''A friend asked me to serve on a committee years ago and I just got caught. Naturally, I give most to the work I have served the longest.'' This was the same story, in different words, of each woman interviewed.

Women are not likely to give in response to telephone calls from strangers, under pressure, or unannounced personal visits. They are repulsed by ostentatious expenditures for advertising or literature. And importantly, they disdain those organizations which fail to say ''thank you.''

There is a general feeling that a woman cannot solicit a significant gift from a man. There are notable exceptions to this. Mrs. Charles Lowrey is considered one of the shrewdest and one of the most persistent fund raisers in San Francisco. ''I hate to see Mimi coming. I know it will cost me plenty. She's hard to refuse.'' Mimi Lowrey has some improtant assets working in her behalf. She is extremely well connected, moves socially in the highest circles, and serves on a number of prestigious boards. She is a doer and respected and recognized as one of the hardest workers in any organization in which she gets involved. She gives unstintingly of her time. Two other factors are of major consequence. When she believes in a program, she makes a consequential gift herself. And in addition to that, when she asks for a gift, she aims at a level of major proportions. She goes for the flinch!

Take the campaign in Bay City, Michigan. We had problems from the beginning. We went after one of the top leaders in the community for the chairmanship of the campaign. He wasn't able to take it. We went after our second choice, but he didn't accept it either. We had an emergency session with the board. We were in trouble. From the group, it was decided that Mrs. Richard Smith should accept the chairmanship. She turned into a miracle worker. The campaign was an overwhelming success. There were some major factors working for Joyce Smith. For starters, she and her attorney husband made a sacrificial gift to the campaign. That was a key element. She was, also, very well known and highly regarded in the community. She was a doer. And one thing more. She was courageous. She could open any door and she was willing to ask for a gift at the proper level.

Sara Blanding was president of Vassar College during some of the years of its most important growth. She was a woman of daring convictions. During the Truman-Dewey presidental campaign for instance, she was the only major college or university president who publicly announced for Truman. Now that took a heap of Kentucky conviction. She was an absolute joy to accompany on a call. She knew how to listen. Didn't miss a word. And then at the right moment, she somehow seemed to know how much to ask and what to ask for. She was a marvel. She was considered one of the most extraordinary fund raisers of her time. Conviction. Integrity. And strategist supreme. She set new standards in higher education, particularly among colleges for women. And she aimed high.

It is interesting to note that the founders of major foundations are almost always men. Remarkable men. None of the major foundations have been started by women. And also of note, nearly all of the men who founded major foundations or who have given large gifts came from very poor beginnings or near-poverty.

Arthur Rubloff says that it does not matter to him whether it is a man or a woman who makes the call but if they are expecting an important gift, the organization had better send an important person. The chances are, man or woman, that if it isn't an important person, they won't even get the appointment. Dmitri George has about the same reaction. He says that it's difficult to get an appointment with him and for some people, downright impossible. "A woman would have the hardest time of all."

W. Clement Stone says that it makes no difference to him whether it is a woman or a man who makes the call. "The trouble is that some of the women aren't trained properly. They haven't learned to tug at the heartstrings. You've got to appeal to the emotions. You've got to get me to cry."

*   *   *   *   *

Dr. Cecil Green, co-founder of Texas Instruments, has given away well over $100 million, mostly since his retirement. In most cases he confers with his wife Ida before making the final decision. Most of the gifts are designated as coming from both Cecil and Ida Green. A partnership of giving.

Frances Mason points out that major gifts were, without exception, made jointly by husband and wife. There was always a discussion between the two of them regarding the size of the gift. Between them, the need of the organization became the major factor determining the amount of the gift. If it was a special capital project, together they decided to increase what they had been doing annually—often tripling their annual contribution.

Leo Beranek says that he always talks to his wife about their gifts. There is no exception to this. And all of the gifts are given in both names. Alex Spanos discusses all of his giving with his wife. Leo Roon always talks with Ann about requests for a gift and together they decide on what will be done.

Homer Watkins makes a number of small gifts on his own but says that he would not consider making a major gift without first talking with his wife. In the Simmerly family, the money came from a large inheritance to Dorothy Simmerly. The positions are somewhat reversed but the concept is the same: "I talk with my husband all the time about my giving. He's very supportive and encouraging. In the end, however, although we tend to agree on most of my giving, the final decision is mine."

One of the phenomena of philanthropy is that where there is giving from both husband and wife, the husband's giving is inevitably larger. This trend has slowly changed in recent years, but the favorite charities of the husband still tend to dominate. That helps explain in part why YMCAs raise more money than YWCAs. Why Boy

Scouts raise more money then Girl Scouts, and why the husband's alma mater receives a larger gift than the wife's.

It is evident that husbands and wives give major gifts in partnership. A call is made, material is left, a request is made. Then the husband and wife talk about the project in detail. Jim Gamble says that not only does he discuss the gift with his wife but that the whole family becomes involved.

But in the majority of cases, the romancing, the interpretation, the call itself is made on only one, most often the husband. If it truly is a joint decision, and the evidence seems to support this, then would there not be great advantages to arranging a call on both the husband and wife? How much easier to make the final sale.

A large number of those interviewed felt that men tend to be more receptive to a major gift than women. There are years of philanthropic tradition that have contributed to this. It is possible, also, that women are concerned with the persistent question of financial security. But the change is taking place and women are accepting greater responsibility for family giving.

The plain fact is that an organization would be much closer to the source and the final decision if they talked to both the husband and wife at the same time.

James S. Copley was unquestionably one of San Diego's leading citizens. He was involved in a major way in every important community endeavor. He and his wife discussed every request for a large gift. When Mr. Copley died, his wife Helen stepped forward to fill the void. She is selective about the trusteeships she accepts and the gifts she makes, but she now occupies a position of leadership in San Diego as significant as the one her husband once held.

* * * * *

The opportunity for memorial giving was rated low by those who were interviewed. But in actuality, most were willing to identify their gift with a memorial or a living tribute. Some did not seek it and others did it because they felt it would encourage future donors to follow. Few refused the opportunity.

Virginia Piper enjoys the recognition she receives. "The opportunities for memorials are important to me, but not for my own sake. I like the thought that I can do something in the name of my husband. There is a bit of ego involved in that. I appreciate the kind of recognition and an appropriate acknowdgement of what I have done. I believe that the acknowledgement of a gift and how it is done can be of great importance. And I am always disappointed if I feel it isn't done properly."

Quite often, a memorial designation does not honor the donor. It is given for a loved one. In the case of Foster McGaw, there is a compelling drive to memorialize his gift by paying honor to his father and mother. W. Clement Stone feels the same way about memorializing others. He will often choose someone who has been an inspiration to him. In some families there is the heritage of giving. From one generation to another, the tradition is handed down. In these instances the children will often memorialize their parents. DeWitt Wallace and his wife, co-founders of *Reader's Digest,* have been generous in extraordinary proportions. There have been many gifts of a million dollars or more. They have allowed their name to be associated with the gifts. In their early philanthropy, however, they especially honored Mr. Wallace's father, a missionary.

John Detwiler had a great love for the sea. He had long planned a spectacular two weeks of scuba diving on the remote island of Palowan. Three weeks after graduating from medical school, his dream became a reality. On the first day of that fateful adventure while exploring a sunken freighter, John disappeared. They searched for him for two days. They finally gave up. Five days later his body washed ashore. He had drifted fifteen miles. He had hoped one day to build and equip a Chinese junk to start medical missionary work in the needy areas of the Southern Philippines. To honor the memory of this young doctor, and to fulfill the lost promise of medical help, his parents have given a million dollars to establish a medical school at the Philippine Union College. John's father, Howard, also a physician, has a great love for the Filipino people. His thought in making the gift was to continue the unfulfilled work of his son. It was a memorial gift, no doubt about it. And one with a deeply moving and spiritual basis.

Institutions have become tastefully ingenious about memorializing gifts. Buildings are an obvious possibility. Endowing chairs at a university. Hospital wings. YMCA swimming pools. Hospital rooms. Individual chairs in an auditorium. Sara Blanding said that she often had no idea what a potential donor's interest was until she made a presentation. Then she would watch for when the tail began to wag! That quickly became the focus of a memorial gift. In the case of the National

College of Education in Evanston, Illinois, most of the buildings were already named. During a campaign for endowment, Foster McGaw was approached for a major gift. He gave over $4 million to the endowment program. To honor the contribution, the College built a small gatepost at its main entrance to the campus and named it in honor of Mr. McGaw. Not a wall, just a gate and post. But it was indeed a memorable way to honor a special benefactor.

*   *   *   *   *

Interviewees did not give a high relationship to their giving and their past involvement in an institution. All indications, however, are to the contrary. College and university campaigns are studded with major gifts from grateful alumni. Hospitals, with gifts from grateful patients. Dortch Oldham gave a million dollars to the University of Richmond. As a student, he had nothing but sheer determination. He earned every penny that went for his tuition and living expenses. "The University turned me around. Changed my life. I always wanted to do something to somehow repay them. I finally had my chance." Marianne Mori gives a great deal of money to her schools. "In this case, I give out of appreciation. I am truly grateful for what they've done for me." George Pardee feels that the reason he has given so much to Scouting and remained involved is that he had such a great experience with the organization as a youth. "My great love is the Boy Scouts. I've been a scouter all my life. I'm on the National Board now. I think that my experience as a youngster has a great deal to do with my maintaining an interest in the program.''

In capital programs for youth organizations and prep schools, parents become prime prospects for major gifts. So do grandparents. The same is obviously true for colleges. Charles Stuart Mott, the mastermind behind the organization of General Motors and a philanthropist of note, had high hopes of his son attending Stevens Institute in Hoboken. The admission requirements, however, were stringent and young Mott was rejected. Instead, he went to the Massachusetts Institute of Technology. Shortly afterwards, Mott gave a multi-million dollar gift to MIT.

9
THE SPIRITUAL, SELFISH, AND STIMULATING

"All you have shall some day be given; therefore, give now that the season of giving may be yours and not your inheritor's."

—Kahlil Gibran
"The Prophet"

THE EAST LIBERTY Presbyterian Church is a magnificent edifice. It is an extraordinary Gothic structure of cathedral proportions. It is on one of the busy streets in a section of Pittsburgh, Pennsylvania. Andrew Mellon, who gave all of the money for the construction, is entombed there. No one knows for certain what motivated the gift for the church. Was it out of guilt? Was it for his love of the church? He had not been known previously as a particularly active layman. Was it because there was a great need for a church in East Liberty? No, there was already a large church there. What part did guilt play? No one knows for certain, but the church is commonly referred to as "Mellon's Fire Escape."

Not one who was interviewed mentioned guilt as a major factor in their giving. It rated the very lowest of all criteria. Louise M. Davies says, "I feel absolutely no guilt and therefore do not give for this reason. But I do feel a very strong sense of duty and obligation. Without question, I feel that it is my responsibility to give and much of what I do is for this reason. Responsibility. Not guilt."

Orwell's view was that rich men feel about their wealth like a dog does gnawing over a stolen leg of mutton. But Dorothy Simmerly doubts that. "I suppose guilt is a factor in some giving, but I think that this is really quite minor. I suspect that there are some who feel that making the large gift does tend to buy yourself a place in heaven. But I can't accept that as a major factor. I have personally never thought of it that way."

One school of psychiatry believes that every action is a reflection of selfish motives. It is possibly true that there is no such thing as a completely selfless gift. If the donor, for instance, takes any special satisfaction in making the gift that is completely anonymous and completely without recognition at all—a gift for the sheer sake of giving, for the satifaction of knowing they are doing good—is not this type of philanthropy an act of self-indulgence? The school of psychiatry to which I refer would say that the gift is selfish to the degree that it provides more complete satisfaction than might seem totally appropriate for a selfless gesture.

Dr. Sigmund Freud says that it remains an open question whether there is such a thing as a genuinely altruistic reaction to one's fellow man, in which the gratification of one's own instincts plays no part at all. This is true even if it is in some displaced or subliminated form. In any case, it is certain that identification is not the only means of acquiring an attitude which has every appearance of altruism.

Lord Baldwin gave back to England, through his will, a fifth of his huge estate, one of the largest in the country at that time. The gift was prompted by a sense of guilt from the profits his steel mills made from the war. Nobel established his prize because of the great devastation he felt he had dealt on humanity through his invention of dynamite. Certainly some givers are convinced that their "good works" will earn them God's special blessing and believe their wealth is a gift of God which must be returned to serve His purposes. This is almost certainly the motivation behind the giving of John D. Rockefeller. Dorothy Simmerly says: "I may be different than other people in their giving. In my case, the money is all mine. I have no one else who I have to consider, no one I have to check with. It's mine to do with as I choose. When I give, it is through no sense of guilt. Absolutely not."

George Delacorte, the millionaire founder of one of America's biggest paperback book publishers, believes that wealthy people should concentrate their talents on giving money away. He says: "In the last few years, I have more or less given up the business. I felt I should devote my time to dying poor. When I die, I shall turn to my wife and say, 'Give it to the pall bearers.' A man should spend as many years of his life as he can in accumulating money, and then, I think he's a jackass if he doesn't spend the rest of it giving it away.''

* * * * *

Arthur Frantzreb has few parallels in the fund raising field. He is one of the great philosophers in the business. The former president of Bard College, Reamer Kline, told me that when Art Frantzreb speaks, it should be engraved in stone. Frantzreb says: "All donors are people. Whether business or foundation executives, alumni, patients, or friends, they have feelings. They also have prejudices. They have ideals. They have fears. But even more, they have a spirit. The act of philanthropy is a spiritual act—an act of love expressed for one's fellow man.'' "Philanthropy'' comes from two Greek words, the *love* of *man*. Frantzreb says that the motivation of giving is an intangible act. The persons who share the resources they own or control buy pride in identification, satisfaction, and accomplishment and in promise for the future.

There is a definite spiritual motivation to most of Foster McGaw's giving. When he and Mrs. McGaw gave $1 million each to thirty-two small colleges about ten years ago, one of the criteria was that the school represent the best in Christian ethics—moralities that the McGaws believe in. The seed was planted firmly by McGaw's father, a Presbyterian missionary. Another stipulation was that the colleges were to be dedicated to the principle of self-help. The McGaws are great believers in character building, self-drive, and motivation. They gave $4 million to the National College of Education because they felt the school was doing an extraordinary job of training teachers who would in turn mold the character and build the fiber of the future citizens of this nation. This was the great motivating factor for this gift. There was a spiritual quality to the donation.

When W. Clement Stone makes a gift, he feels that he is really doing the Lord's work, sharing his time, expertise, and wealth. ''A spiritual influence is always present in my giving. I feel that when I give, I am directed.'' He says that anyone who has been raised with a religious background tends to help worthy causes. It is something that is ingrained in the soul. Virginia Piper says, ''There is a definite relationship between giving and the joy I find in my life. I feel I live my religion and I do that through my giving—it's the way I share with others. There is great fulfillment and reward. In that sense there is a definite spiritual motivation to my gifts.''

At best, the statistics on philanthropy are imprecise. Last year, for instance, giving to religion constituted by far the major source of philanthropy's direction. It represented 46¢ out of every dollar of the total philanthropy in the nation. In the case of church-related colleges and church-related hospitals, the contributions were counted toward education and health, not religion. Without question in the case of many donors, the motivating factor and the most compelling for giving would be a religious one— but directed toward the college and hospital. As a general rule, large donors feel deeply about religion and spiritual matters. Not necessarily focused through a church but deeply spiritual nonetheless.

The spiritual factor is an important one, although not easy to describe and not readily identified by those who were interviewed. Not necessarily religious or churchy, but spiritual in the sense of altruistic. Driven by the desire to do something for the common good, a better order, a higher need.

Very often, it is difficult or impossible to distinguish the spiritual or religious motivation which compels a donor to a particular cause. Take for instance the medical center of Oral Roberts University. It is estimated that over $200 million has been contributed to date toward that controversial, non-approved, state-condemned institution. Sizable gifts were made. Were they gifts for healthcare, in support of the University, or for a religious reason? An even closer look is worthwhile. It is a fascinating project, one which could not have been undertaken without the greatest faith possible.

The Tulsa Hospital Council and the Oklahoma Health Systems Agency had disapproved the project, almost out of hand. Tulsa already had far too many hospital beds. They said to Oral Roberts: "You will not be allowed to build your hospital." Oral Roberts said: "I shall."

According to Dr. Roberts, building the City of Faith, as his medical center is known, was divinely inspired. His daughter had just died and his grief was without bounds. Even his great faith was tested beyond limits. He could not overcome the overwhelming weight of the loss. While he was in prayer Roberts claims that God appeared and said: "Oral Roberts, I want you to build a great medical center, a city of faith, a center of healing and health for all My followers." And Roberts said: "I am Your servant but there is no way that I can build such a costly institution." And God said to him: "You can't. But I can. I will build it through you and it will be built debt free." I assume that this was partly a result of God having to deal in the past with lenders and mortgage bankers! The medical center is staffed with physicians drawn from all over the country who have the same fundamentalist faith as Oral Roberts. The nursing staff and all other employees are also of the same religious persuasion. It is indeed an extraordinary mix of bottomless faith and spiritual generosity.

Some time has passed, bringing reports that the medical complex is in dire financial trouble. Coincidentally, Oral Roberts had another visit. This time, Jesus appeared to him in person. "I want you to find a cure for cancer." This medical research was to be financed by "prayer partners"—followers of Roberts who would make gifts of $240 a person. Thus far, over $5 million has been raised toward this crusade.

A spiritual impulse and drive. Not necessarily religious, Andrew Carnegie felt that philanthropy was a social obligation incumbent on the rich. More than that, and of greater importance, he felt it was a religious duty. Yet, he gave virtually none of his money for strictly religious programs. To him, religion was a more generic term and had very little to do with the formal, structured church. In his lifetime, he provided the funds for 7,689 church organs, but that was only because he loved music. He was not religious himself. Foster G. McGaw feels that his giving, in a major way, is a manner of "making a repayment" and showing appreciation. "God has been so very good to me and in return, I must be good in sharing my resources with people. I owe Him that."

*   *   *   *   *

I learned my early lessons in fund raising from some wonderful volunteers and a number of major donors. They were great teachers all. Clement Stone was one of them. Much of his philanthropy is in the form of challenge gifts, motivating others to do more and reach higher. Stone says: "I most often make challenge gifts and I do think that this encourages others. Recently, on one of my projects, we were coming near the end of the program and they hadn't raised the money to meet my challenge. I said to them, 'Look, a deal's a deal. If you don't raise it, you don't get my gift.' In a week they went out and raised the whole amount, and then some. I have been an exponent of the challenge gift for years." The plain fact is, however, that on the basis of my discussions with the million dollar givers, I doubt that it is as important a factor as I had thought. James Gamble feels that it is important at times to give a challenge gift and he has found it effective to promote a joint challenge, where two or three donors get together and provide the challenge. "But I also find that while it sometimes works, sometimes it doesn't. I don't find, on my own part, that I feel keenly about responding to a challenge gift that someone else has made. I have either decided to give to that organization or not and the challenge gift has little influence on that."

"Being a woman," says Dorothy Simmerly, "and being in a business that is all mine, that isn't dependent on any friends or other associates for my business, I don't need to match anyone's giving. I really don't care what others do and how they feel about my philanthropy. I don't respond to challenges and I don't offer them. I don't think it has much of an impact." Louise M. Davies says that there are some people who simply don't give and challenges would mean nothing to them. In her experience, large donors don't respond to challenges, either. She does feel, however, that large gifts establish a pattern for other donors. She felt that this was true in the case of the $5 million she gave to the Center for the Performing Arts. "Mine was one of the early gifts. It wasn't a challenge, but I feel it helped motivate others to do as much as they could. It set the pattern. I didn't expect anyone to match my gift but I thought that it would be encouraging to them and to the project. I think it was." Homer Watkins is more direct. "I don't care what others do. I wouldn't change my thinking regarding a gift whether there was a challenge or not. And I don't think it motivates others."

Cyril Magnin says, "I don't worry much about what others give. It is not a consideration in my own giving. I don't respond any differently to challenges. If I'm interested in the program, I'm interested. If not, the challenge doesn't motivate me. I think that what others do is up to them. People should lead their own lives. I have enough trouble worrying about mine. I don't necessarily understand why some people who have money don't give more, but I never blame them. They ought to do what they want to. I don't think a challenge has much effect and as far as I'm concerned, it turns me off"

On a number of occasions, I have found the challenge gift to be a valuable concept. In the case of one college campaign, we went to see the largest potential donor first of all. We had prepared well. It was an excellent presentation. The only problem was that the donor had pretty much made up his mind as to the size of the gift.

It was a good one, but only about half the size of what we had hoped. Before leaving the session, it was suggested that the donor give what he had planned, but that he double the donation if the campaign was successful. He seemed interested. We asked for permission to announce this ''added'' gift which would be forthcoming if everyone did their share. The campaign was successful and we received the bonus. A number of combinations follow the same scenario. In countless successful campaigns a challenge helped put the program over. But very seldom did it inspire large donors. DeWitt Wallace gave the Girls Clubs of America a million dollars if they would raise an equal amount. They had just completed a successful campaign several years before, but his challenge encouraged them to start again. They did, and they were successful.

10
ARE YOU DOZING THROUGH A CHANGING MARKET?

"Every donor should look to his own purpose and problems, which are not necessarily those of the institution. Even in philanthropy, the customer is usually right, and his judgment can be just as thoughtful, long range, and in the public interest as those of the recipient. Often more so."

—Kenneth Patrick

LORILLARD WAS having a disastrous time promoting its full-flavored cigarettes. What was happening, of course, was that the market was changing. There began to be a perceptible shift in consumer attitudes about smoking. People were kicking the habit. Even those who were still smoking were starting to become aware of those low tar numbers. Lorillard continued their heavy promotion. Macho men, tattoos, western scenes, the works. Still, their sales plummeted. Finally, they conducted a market study. "Those tests opened our eyes," recounts Curt Judge, head of Lorillard. Finally, we got wise enough to say, hell, let's give them what they want." This was the first step Lorillard made in turning its losses into profits. They began pushing the low tars. It was as simple as that. They began giving smokers what they wanted.

Two hundred years before, Benjamin Franklin had the same type of problem in selling his product. To induce the French to join the young colony in its fight against the English, a stream of official representatives called on the French to convince them of how their participation in the war would be to their commercial advantage and enhance their trade and business. The new country would import only from France. To no avail. The French were unmoved. Franklin knew better. He touched the right button. He understood that the French were a passionate people, moved more by their heart than their pocket. They were not interested in commerce or trade. "France is truly a generous nation and gracious people, fond of glory, and particularly interested in protecting the oppressed. Trade is not the admiration of their people. We must appeal to their highest and most noble motivations. Telling them that their commerce will be advantaged by our victory seems to say: help us and we shall not be obliged to you." Franklin was a master marketer. He sold the French on helping the underdog, the oppressed. He sold liberty and honor. And France joined the Revolution.

Securing a large gift is often a case of good marketing. You help the donor share in the dream, and decide for himself what he wishes to give you.

Dale Carnegie had a favorite story he enjoyed telling. He recounted how he went fishing in Maine every summer. "I'm very fond of strawberries and cream. But I find for some strange reason, fish prefer worms. So when I go fishing, I don't think about what I want, I think about what the fish want. I don't bait the hook with strawberries and cream. Rather, I dangle a worm or a grasshopper in front of the fish and I say—wouldn't you like to have that?''

Why not use the same common sense as Dale Carnegie when you are fishing for men? Or fishing for a gift?

There are men and women out there, waiting to be asked to give to your cause. Major donors. There are men and women of immense personal resources, greater than ever before in our history. They are waiting for the right opportunity and a great dream for their personal, quiet, spiritual, and philanthropic commitment. Few actions of consequence in the world have been accomplished without passion. Securing a large gift is not the result of mechanical procedures and routinized presentations. It is the drama. The excitement. The passion.

Securing the large gift is the art of human relations and persuading potential donors. But to win them to your cause you must follow the time-tested marketing adage—give them more and more of what they want and less and less of what they don't want. That doesn't mean at all that you have to settle for a designated gift that is not relevant to the mission of your organization or one that is not in keeping with the program of the campaign. Good marketing means helping the major donor want to share in your dream. This means proper interpretation and effective persuasion. And you listen. You really listen. You hear what his hopes and aspirations are for the organization. You find a way of helping him make his design fit your objective. If you don't, you won't get a gift. If you persist in selling your idea, one in which he is not particularly interested, you won't get the gift.

Homer Watkins says that he is tired of organizations that try to sell him their bill of goods. "They come marching in here with their ideas and their fancy proposals. They don't ask what I'm interested in. They are only interested in telling me what they want me to buy. It is impossible for me to get involved in that kind of a situation." Dorothy Simmerly reports that she's extremely choosy about her giving. "I love to give, but I am picky about the organization which I choose. They had better know what I am interested in before they come calling on me."

Long ago, the toothpaste companies learned their lesson. Brushing teeth and using dental floss is a nuisance, a plain pain. Long ago, Colgate learned that the way to sell toothpaste was to promise beauty, an alluring smile, and romance. Large donors do not give to needy causes. Worthy organizations. They give to dreams, to visions, to bold and imaginative ventures. They give to projects in which they are interested. In which they have had an opportunity in designing the program.

Charles Lazarus is the creative genius behind Toys 'R' Us. He built the largest retail system of playthings in the United States. He says that it was soon after opening his first juvenile furniture store in his father's former bicycle shop that he learned the first lesson in business. Don't sell what you want. Sell what they want.

Too often in fund raising, the programs we know with great clarity that might be the most important to our program are irrelevant to the major donor. The trick is making your dream his. And if it appears to be his idea, all the better. The secret of securing a large gift is vision, imagination, and intellect all brought together at one point. Your job is to help the major donor bring all of these ingredients together for your cause. That's the genius of the mega gift—making your vision and dream the donor's. William James said that genius is sometimes nothing more than ''simply looking at things a different way.''

* * * * *

One day, in 1980, Edwin C. "Jack" Whitehead discovered he was a wealthy man. A very wealthy man. He sold his company Technicon to Revlon for $400 million in stock and cash. Not bad for a young man who started out as the company's $10 a week shipping clerk. Not bad for a bored and restless youngster who left college after one year. An extraordinary man, Jack Whitehead. A tough competitor, impeccable standards of ethics, and an uncompromising drive for excellence.

His recent gift to establish the Whitehead Institute in affiliation with the Massachusetts Institute of Technology represents the second largest gift ever made by a living person in the history of the United States. $120 million. Add to that a gift of $10 million to Duke University. And $1 million to the Hastings Center, an institute devoted to the study of society, ethics, and the life sciences. He is intense, and tough. He loves to take risks, ski, live, and laugh. Not necessarily in that order. In conversation, he doesn't seem to take himself too seriously and money is not an obsession in his life. Perhaps it does not need to be if you have $400 million! He says that money has *never been terribly important to him—it is the fuel, not the engine of life. On one hand a visionary, on the other a pragmatist. He prefers his truth and his conversation unvarnished. He believes that society is made up of givers and takers. He doesn't have much time for takers. He's a man in a hurry, and life is an adventure.*

People do not give cerebrally. They give emotionally. *"Un coup de fondre,"* say the French. Literally, "a strike of lightning"—love at first sight. Edwin Whitehead says that he believes that most of his giving is rational and well-considered. But he is certain that most gifts are emotional. To give breath and life to the dream, most organizations start with campaign literature, magnificent brochures, five-color pieces, catchy and heartrending themes.

As far as the major donor is concerned, experience and my interviews indicate clearly that this type of selling is most often ineffective. At times, counter-productive. Too often, sophisticated or fancy campaign literature has as much impact as the sound of one hand clapping.

Frances Mason reported that women she interviewed were not untouched by the well-known competition for the philanthropic dollar. They did not respond well to highly emotional appeals or any form of intense pressure. They seemed to be unaffected by mail appeals, by publicity carried in the media, or by campaign literature. Her donors were unimpressed by handsome brochures, "good" paper, or a score of illustrations. The fancy folder often irritated them. A simple presentation was much more respected than the pamphlet that looked expensive.

Alex Spanos says that most campaign material is a waste of time. ''It really turns me off. The fancier it is, the angrier I get. People tell you that they just throw the stuff in the waste basket. Well, I do.''

Marianne McDonald Mori is in her early forties and very attractive. She has earned a doctorate in Classical Studies and the head of the department who monitored her work and thesis says that Marianne is possibly one of the brightest who have gone through the school. She lives with her Japanese husband on 27 acres in Southern California, along with a horde of children, several peacocks, a number of dogs, and an assortment of other animals and birds of all sizes and varieties. She is filled with curiosity and she has a wide range of interests. Marianne is not a softie or a sentimentalist, but hearing about the troubles and problems of a youngster can bring tears.

Her father was founder of the Zenith Radio Corporation and she had used that inheritance for a number of entrepreneurial and philanthropic endeavors. Her recent gift to the University was the largest in its history and at the time it was made and up to the writing of this book, it was an anonymous gift. She is a prodigious worker, extremely well organized, and delegates her time with the skill of a business executive. She is heavily involved in the Greek Orthodox Church, studies Buddhism, practices yoga, trains at fencing, and is on the faculty of the University. And that's only one day's activity.

''Some campaign material really puts me off,'' says Mrs. Mori. ''I hate the feeling that a lot of money has been spent to convince me of something. That's not the best way to convince me of anything. I think that fancy material is counterproductive.''

Dortch Oldham feels that campaign literature is essential but that it must be kept very simple and very direct. Fancy material bothers him and has the wrong impact. Leo Beranek says, ''Campaign literature has zero influence on me. It simply has no influence at all. As far as I'm concerned, that is not the way to reach me or sell a program.'' Cyril Magnin concurs. ''Campaign material means virtually nothing to me. If you want to get my gift, you have to get to the point and capture my interest. It has to have appeal but be simple. If it looks like too much money has been spent on the presentation, I have a negative reaction. The material really doesn't sell me.'' James Gamble feels that literature has little impact on major donors but that it is important for smaller gifts. ''I'm never motivated by the literature of a campaign—it simply doesn't affect me one way or the other. Even the literature that I prepare myself!''

Virginia Piper says that campaign material has absolutely no impact on her. It never influences the gifts that she makes. There is no end to the number of presentations W. Clement Stone has heard, or the amount of campaign literature he has seen. But he says that the material isn't important to him at all. ''I have given to a lot of programs where I have bought a dream and a vision. No written material at all.'' Arthur Rubloff says that he is so tired of the campaign folders he sees that they really turn him off. ''And the fancier the material, the more turned off I get. I don't think this is really the way you raise money.''

The question is, how do you get your story across

effectively? For the major donor, you do it as simply as possible. And as personally as possible, directed to the donor's particular interest and concern. Sell your program, but make certain it is something the donor wants to buy. It is possible that you show no material at all until after the first or second visit. You talk about your institution. Its special mission. How it serves a need unmet by any other organization. How your campaign program can meet both the objectives of the organization and the wishes of the donor. You talk, but if you are smart, you listen. The donor has needs also.

Among the group I interviewed, it was clear. The megagivers want to be loved, admired, respected, and remembered favorably. And also just as true, they want to serve mankind and feel that their gift is used for the most consequential good possible. They want value for their money. After you truly understand the needs of the donor, and only after that, are you in a position to present precisely the proper campaign literature.

What is clear through all of the interviews is that the motivating factors are different for each person. Each project elicits a distinctive mix of motivational impulses, even from the same donor. The same candle that sets off a blaze can also be used to melt butter.

Campaign literature is certainly important. It states officially the dimensions of the program. The solicitor should use it to cement a verbal presentation. It is probably effective for smaller gifts. But for the major donor, it will likely take something different to make the sale.

In the past few years, we have used a different approach with extraordinary results. For the potential major donor, we have a presentation which is tailor-made to that donor's particular interests. This is usually developed and designed after several discussions. The material is often very long. A thoughtful gift deserves a thoughtful presentation. One that is detailed and responds to every possible question. It also provides proof of the thought and concern that went into the presentation. Usually, a one-page summary pulls it and the request together.

"Keep it brief" are not necessarily the watch-words. How long should a presentation be? As long as it needs to be! A full and thorough review of the program is important. Attach a brief summary to take the curse off of the length. Some of our most impressive and effective presentations have been typed and placed in a three-ring binder—usually studded with captivating and appropriate photographs.

Among those I interviewed, we spoke about thirty-one specific gifts of a million dollars or more. Among that group, only three donors acted on a printed campaign brochure, and in the case of these three, the printed folder was of little influence. It was the verbal presentation that made the difference. Many of the gifts were made without any campaign material at all and the balance had tailor-made presentations. "I need to know why they want me to give to their programs," said Amon Carter. "Me, particularly."

11
THE RESPONSE IS SPONTANEOUS

"What great things would you attempt if you knew you could not fail?"

—*Robert Fuller*

IT WAS a fascinating story.

Alex Spanos lives in Stockton, California. That's a couple of hours away from San Francisco, if you drive fast. It's a world away in almost every other respect. Alex Spanos tells me about a telephone call he received recently.

"This lady called, and she said that she is on the board of a museum in San Francisco. She says that she would like me to sponsor the 'Search for Alexander' exhibit and she wants to know if I would be interested in sharing in the cost." Alex says that it took him exactly ten seconds to make the decision. The moment he heard the idea, he was excited about it and decided to go ahead. "I thought it was a great idea, and expressed a part of my heritage. On top of all of that, I was named for Alexander. Everything just fit into place. I don't believe I found out until much later what the cost was—it was a quarter of a million. But that really wasn't important to me. The idea was right and it was right for me." Mr. Spanos tells how he said to the solicitor, whom he has gotten to know quite well by now, that he would sponsor the exhibit. There was a l-o-n-g silence. And then almost in disbelief: "Er, Mr. Spanos, would you be interested in knowing anything more or what the cost would be?" The gift was made and delivered. On the spot. Spontaneously.

All gifts are not made that quickly. You can count on that. It is my experience, however, strongly confirmed by the million dollar givers, that major philanthropy is spontaneous. They may not make the actual gift or sign the pledge card for months, but in their minds they have pretty much made their decision as to whether they will support the program or not.

Donors are going to support the program, or they are not. The juices are flowing and they are excited. You hear the sound and flourish of trumpets. The program really is something that they want to share in, feel strongly about, are in enthusiastic sympathy. All that remains is to tie it down, determine the level of giving, work on the proper timing.

I am now so convinced that there is an almost "immediate click," that I have done a great deal of thinking about some of the important potential gifts I have worked on in the past that never materialized. I am certain now that it follows the old legal axiom "to doubt and delay is to deny."

A thoughtful donor will certainly wish to talk to his or her spouse about a gift. If it is in the range of "major proportions," an attorney or accountant will certainly be consulted. This takes time. That is not the kind of delay I refer to.

I have been involved in many campaigns where some of our top prospects have put us off, refused to make a decision, or have indicated that we should see them in six months or so. We hung on to those prospects for dear life and in some cases they were our major hope. As I look back, virtually none of those gifts materialized. Now that I think about it, I realize that there was not the spark, the excitement. No awe or wonder. No trumpets. And in most cases, we were guilty of talking and not listening.

The chances are almost certain that you will not receive a meaningful answer or a consequential gift on the first visit. If you think you have, you are almost always wrong. The chances are, you could have gotten more! If, on the other hand, you have made several calls, including what you consider to be a solid presentation, and you don't see some of the vital signals, you had better begin thinking of a different strategy. Perhaps you had better request a delay or a postponement in the decision. "I'd like to wait until things get better." "Not right now, maybe later." "I'll see what my attorney says and get back to you in a couple of months." These are almost sure signs that you had better look for another top prospect. You are most likely to be disappointed.

Marianne Mori says, "I give spontaneously. Actually, I think most people do. I know that this sounds terrible but I think that almost all women give the same way. There is a lot of emotion involved in our giving. I find that if I'm spending a great deal of time deciding whether I'm going to give to a certain program or not, something is just not right, and I usually end up not giving. When a program is just right for me I feel it immediately."

Dmitri George is a successful venture capitalist and a daring entrepreneur. He asked that he not be identified. Recently he gave $1 million to a midwest hospital in grateful appreciation for the care his father received. He told me that; "There's no question about it, my giving is spontaneous. I decide on the spot whether I'm interested in the program or not."

Louise M. Davies tells about her $5 million gift to establish the Center for Performing Arts. "I decided as soon as I heard about the project that I was going to give. I had pretty much made up my mind and as a matter of fact, I was fairly well sold on the idea before I was even called on. There was none of that campaign material or a fancy sales call. I pretty much made up my mind on the spot. The decision was made quickly. When the question was finally asked as to whether I would consider a gift, I told them immediately what was on my mind. Five million dollars, and that was that. Later, after it was pretty much all done, I went to my tax advisor and banker and told them. Actually, I believe they may have thought me a bit naughty, not to have checked with them first. But I did it from my heart, not for tax reasons.

"Actually, when I think back on it, making the gift was not the result of a momentous decision or anything like that. It took me virtually no time to think it through. I have the money and I decided that my children have enough. I decided I was going to give it away. As soon as I heard about the program I knew immediately that was for me. I was going to make the gift. I wasn't certain at the time what the size would be, but I knew it would be large. I wanted to do something really special."

Virginia Piper's comments on this particular subject are revealing and help confirm my "to doubt or delay is to deny" thesis. "I don't want to be pushed by some overbearing person trying to make me give a gift. I've got to feel that I'm making my own decision. I find that if I'm taking an unduly long time in making a decision, I've probably decided not to give.

"A program triggers an emotional response in me quickly. I begin getting the feeling almost spontaneously as to whether I am going to make a gift or not. If it appears to be positive then I begin a very thorough process of checking the institution out. But by then, I have pretty much decided I am going to give. It is just a question of the amount."

She talks further about the part her emotions play in her giving. "I think that women are far more emotional in their giving than men. I know that I am. When someone talks with me about a project, I make a decision almost immediately as to whether I shall consider supporting it or not. And this is almost an emotional decision. If I decide to look at it further, I do some careful checking—but it's the emotional decision which comes first. My giving is almost entirely emotional. I think I'm a very sensitive person and I react emotionally to the needs of people. I even cry at movies! When I am asked to make a gift, I react emotionally. I'm interested, for instance, in the needs of the elderly. I'm very sensitive to this group. When a program comes up for the elderly, if it's something important at all, I have an emotional reaction. It happens quickly, almost spontaneously.''

W. Clement Stone has made a number of gifts of a million dollars or more. In business, he is a man of action. In giving, he reacts the same. "My giving is spontaneous. I decide right away what I'm going to do. Once having made the decision, I do check it out pretty well, and my staff checks it out extremely well and makes certain that it is a worthwhile program. I make a decision pretty quickly on whether I am going to make a gift or not. When a person calls on me, it's what they say and how they say it. That's when I decide what I'm going to do and that is very, very important. If I find that I feel that I've got to take time to think it over that usually means that I have decided not to make the gift.

Arthur Rubloff says: "It doesn't really take me much time to decide whether I am interested in a program or not. As soon as I hear the story, I've a fairly good idea of whether I'm going to give or not. After that, it doesn't take much time at all to make the decision. That doesn't mean that I'm always right. I've never made a bad real estate deal in my life, but I certainly have had some major disappointments with some of the projects I have contributed to. Mostly, it's been a case of people promising too much. I still feel that my initial instincts are right.''

James Gamble is a person who has studied the psychology and strategy of the business about as much as any volunteer in the field. He says, ''I like to think that I give intellectually, but even in my case I know that the sizzle has a lot to do with the size of my gift. I've got to have the right kind of emotional feeling about the program, and when I do it has a great impact on me. I think that I am pretty tough in analyzing a project. But when it comes right down to it, I often go with the emotions.'' Cyril Magnin is first and foremost a businessman. He says that he really tries to give carefully. ''I try to make certain that the organizations I give to are worthy and that my money is being put to the best use possible. But there is a definite spontaneity to what I do. It takes me virtually no time to decide whether or not I'm interested in the program. I hear the presentation and I think about it thoughtfully, but almost immediately I have decided whether I am going to give or not.'' George Pardee is a self-made man. He has built a fortune on his ability to analyze carefully. Every major business decision was calculated thoughtfully. His giving does not necessarily follow the same pattern. ''There's a lot of emotion in what I give. I think it through, of course; but the emotions play an important part. I sense quite quickly whether the program is for me or not. And my emotions play a significant part in this.''

Large gifts. Really large gifts. These are given emotionally, not cerebrally. And almost always, the decision is made spontaneously. The final commitment may come later but the spark is ignited early.

*   *   *   *   *

People tend to give more to programs in which they have had some involvement. Earl Blackwell is the self-appointed arbitrator of celebrity protocol. Still, on the matter of charity, he speaks with some merit. He says that if you want to seriously make it, "take an active interest in the arts or charity work. Always be willing to work and to donate money to charity. That way, you will be welcome. You can't just send a check and think that that will do it."

Edwin Whitehead says that he's a participator in everything he does. He loves getting involved. And that when he gets involved in a program, he tends to give more.

Leo Beranek tells how he has been interested in music all his life, since he was ten or eleven. His gift to the Boston Symphony—the largest that they had ever received up to that time—came easily to him. "It was very natural for me to be interested in our symphony. I was on the board for almost fifteen years and as a director, I felt encouraged to give a little bit more money. When I was asked to chair the resources committee, I felt I simply had to set a good example. I think that if I hadn't been as heavily involved, I wouldn't have done as much." Edwin Whitehead just gave a million dollars to the Hastings Institute. "What could I do? I was chairman of the fund raising committee. I was involved. I was also terribly interested in what they do. I believe in them. Everything fit together."

For Dorothy Simmerly, it works both ways. "Compassion is the key word. When I am asked to make a gift to a project, I get quite involved. Or when I'm involved in a program, how can I not give generously? I don't waste my time. If I weren't vitally interested, I wouldn't be involved. And if I'm involved, I give.''

Direct involvement in a program—either a past experience or a present participation—isn't a prerequisite for major giving. Nor is it a guarantee. On the other hand, it is unquestionably an important motivating factor. Familiarity breeds favorability. This is a truism you can count on. Large donors have too many ways to spend time and energy. If they are deeply involved in your program, the chances are they will support it. You can be confident of the ''familiarity breeds favorability'' concept. As Mark Twain said: ''With the calm confidence of a Christian with four aces.''

12
WHEN THEY DON'T BELIEVE—THEY DON'T GIVE

"We make a living by what we get, but we make life of what we give."

—Winston Churchill

ARTHUR RUBLOFF may have a heart of gold—by his own admission, he does—but when he talks across the desk from you, he can be plenty tough and gruff. "This fund raiser comes in and is doing a real thing on me. I finally got tired of listening to him. There was nothing he could have said or done that would have motivated me to give to his project, not even a small gift. I simply was not interested at all in the organization or what they were trying to accomplish. For me, that's the most important thing of all in making a gift. I asked him to take a walk."

No single factor rated higher, or was considered to be of greater consequence. To those who make the really large gift, there has to be an unswerving belief in the objectives and the mission of the institution. This takes precedence over any other factor. No matter how tantalizing the project, no matter how persuasive the caller, no matter how distinguished the organization. A dedicated belief in the work and role or the organization is quintessential.

Inevitably, an organization is measured by its consuming objectives, and by the zeal with which it regards its ultimate mission. Large gifts go to the institution with a sense of destiny. ''The mission is crucial as far as I am concerned,'' says Edwin Whitehead. ''The mission is first. I don't care who calls on me, that's second. So many institutions don't have a mission. They won't be able to raise money from me. They won't be able to raise money at all.'' Whitehead concludes by saying that he expects noncompromising quality, the highest of standards, in the institutions he supports. He looks for long term goals. And first and foremost, he must identify with the mission of the organization.

Roberta Deree thinks about the many projects she and her husband could have supported over the years. William Deree was born in Greece and there was no lack of programs there or in this country which needed help. He was wealthy, he was generous, and he was accessible. He served on many boards and he made a number of gifts, but nothing nearly as substantial as his philanthropy to the American College of Greece. Mrs. Deree says that she feels certain that the factor that meant the most to her husband was the feeling that the College had a vital role, a real mission. Something he understood and believed in. It is a school with a future and a purpose.

Because of his special position and role in Fort Worth, Texas, Amon Carter, Jr. tries to give something, even a small gift, to every worthwhile program. But the really large gifts are reserved for those organizations and programs where Carter can identify with the mission. W. Clement Stone says, ''Belief in the institution and its mission is all important to me. I think that it is probably the most important single factor. When you have a goal, it makes everything else in your life easier—even giving. All I want to do is to change the world for now and for all generations. In my giving, I am eager to support organizations that have the same kind of mission that I do. I wouldn't consider giving to something that I didn't believe in. Not even a small gift.''

Leo Roon feels that it would be inconceivable that he would ever make a gift to where he didn't really believe strongly in the institution and its mission. ''I might make a small donation if a friend or a member of my family was involved, but I would have to personally find something quite compelling in the program and its objectives before I would make a significant gift.''

There is no lack of organizations that need help. Large gifts and small. When the mega giver considers a truly significant gift, you must offer assurance that the gift will count for something. That it will make an important difference. In some cases, perhaps benefit all of mankind. Significant gifts are not made to insignificant projects. Nor to institutions whose mission and objectives are not in harmony with that of the donor. Marianne Mori feels that she is a generous giver, ''. . . and

I would like to think that my philanthropy really makes a difference. I want to do something for the good of mankind. I would like to think that my help and influence can really make a difference. There is nothing that could move me to making a large gift if I did not believe in the mission of the organization.''

Someone, out there, is ready to give to your program. Is waiting to be asked and has the resources necessary to make a gift of consequence. Eager to give to the organization whose mission is compelling.

You have selected your top prospect. You have been careful in conducting a thorough analysis of the individual. Thorough research is critical to success. You've discussed who might be the best person possible to make the call, and you feel you are going in with your heaviest guns. You will make a serious mistake, however, if you try to sell a specific project or program and there is no prior knowledge or identification with the organization's mission. This is crucial. You will not get a gift for your specific project. The evidence in this regard is quite clear. You will only succeed if there is a great belief in the role and function of the organization. Sell that foremost. Do not take it for granted, even among those who you feel know you well or best of all. Sell your mission with the most ardor possible. When you feel you have accomplished this you are ready to talk about the campaign program or the specific project.

* * * * *

Not of equal importance, but ranking quite high among the factors that are considered of importance to the large donor, is the financial stability of the institution. Mind you, they are interested, these major donors, in big dreams, bold visions, new horizons. These are seldom identified with organizations with financial problems. Almost always, big donors run away from the institution that has a history of deficits. Why would anyone want to save a sinking ship? That sort of an organization is normally always adrift, in stormy waters, and running aground. No sense of mission, never achieving a high or dramatic set of objectives. Not going anywhere. A small twig, being tossed about in an ocean of waves.

Major donors, also, most often identify the financial stability of an organization with its staff leadership. The executive officer establishes the pace, develops the design, and provides the vitality to the organization. The major donor responds to vital and dynamic staff leadership. Very seldom will they make a large gift to an organization where they cannot identify with an inspired executive staff person. And for the major donor, they relate that type of leadership directly to the financial stability of the organization.

Virginia Piper is eloquent on the subject. She asks, ''Why give to something that is in great difficulty or is having serious financial problems? If there is that kind of a problem, it makes you raise questions about the quality of the organization and its staff. I don't want to be a part of a losing cause. I don't enjoy giving to an organization that is doing poorly. I think that everyone likes to be a part of a winning team. The one ingredient that I look for probably the very most is to make certain that it is a quality institution. Quality, that is the key to me. It is the thing I look for the very most. When you have that in an institution, you can have faith in everything else they do. I want solidarity behind the giving. You want to make certain that the money goes for what it was intended. You want to make certain that it is effectively used and for the right purpose. And that always means having the right staff. And that means integrity and stability.''

Frances Mason points out that donors were unanimously concerned with where their money went. They admired an efficient and realistic administration. Thrift was, in itself, not sought. Few donors were interested in scrutinizing budgets. If they had regard and respect for the administration, donors assumed that funds were being used properly.

Among the mega givers, this was almost always the case. Alex Spanos never questions the financial stability of the institutions he supports. He assumes that there is good staff leadership and good board leadership and they are going to be careful about what they do. If he did not feel this way, he would not support the institution in the first place. ''I don't try to monitor my gift in any way,'' says Arthur Rubloff. ''When I make a gift, I don't track it. I assume that the institution is going to make wise use of the money I give them. If I didn't feel this way and feel good about the staff, the chances are that I would not make the gift to begin with.''

Leo Roon simply won't give to an organization he feels is poorly managed. This is true in virtually every single case of a major gift. I know of no exception. Roon says: ''If I think that an organization is poorly managed or I have some question about it, I just won't give. I can't understand or support poor management.

To me, that would symbolize the poor utilization of my gift. If the management is poor, the chances are almost certain that the board of directors is ineffective. And that would be like throwing your money away.'' Dorothy Simmerly concurs. ''I insist that my money be used wisely. I think that this is terribly essential. If I feel that it has not been spent prudently, you can be certain that the organization won't get another gift. I won't create a fuss. I just won't give again. I'm picky, very picky, about the way my money is spent. I want to make certain that there is great care given to that. I won't give to a poorly managed organization or one which is always in financial trouble.''

While major donors are not interested in a thorough examination of the finances of an institution, they insist that their money is used effectively and wisely. To Homer Watkins, financial instability and poor staff leadership are synonymous. In the case of most donors, this is true. Marianne Mori likes to make certain that a charity is strong and the money is put to good use. ''I have a great concern that the organization knows how to use my gift intelligently. If I respect the institution, it almost always means I respect the staff and the volunteers.''

Donors clearly expect financial stability and strong management in the institutions they support. For the mega donor, it's a dramatic case of the effectiveness of your management and your financial stability speaks so loudly, I can't hear what you say about your fund raising program.

This in a major way helps explain why staff can be so very effective in securing the large gift. Major donors respond to staff. They give to strong, dynamic staffs.

They are inspired. Motivated. Jump over hurdles they never thought possible. They make gifts, often far beyond what they might have initially considered. The effective staff person is an essential factor in the equation.

This also explains in part why the financial stability of an institution is important to the major donor. The big gift is not made because there is a need. Major donors give to major opportunities. The big dreams. Edwin Whitehead feels that an organization in financial trouble is not really capable of making a significant difference. It is spending all of its time and energy simply trying to save itself.

Donors do not want to be part of a rescue mission. They seek a partnership in an exciting venture with a successful institution. It confirms what has been called "The Matthew Syndrome" (St Matthew 25:29): "For unto everyone that hath shall be given, and he shall have abundance; but from him that hath not shall be taken away even that he hath."

13

TAX INCENTIVE IS LITTLE INCENTIVE

"Gain all you can, save all you can, give all you can."

—John Wesley

Take a look. Pick up any organizational brochure or a piece of campaign literature and the chances are almost certain that there will be a major reference to the tax deductibility of a gift. There is often a prominent reference to it in a written and verbal presentation to a potential major donor.

How significant is the matter of tax deductibility? With each major revision of the Tax Law, there has been a handwringing among organizations and predictions of doom. The evidence appears clearly to the contrary.

Tax deductions for charitable gifts were not allowed

prior to 1917. Yet, donors of some of the older and largest foundations preceded that date. In a recent Gallup study, 1,000 heads of households across the country indicated that only 30 per cent itemized their tax returns. Of this group, only 8 per cent said that the tax deduction was a reason for giving. This means that only 24 out of every 1,000 gifts are prompted by tax inducements. As a matter of fact, in another Gallup study it was discovered that only two out of every 1,000 people actually comprehend the tax implications of giving.

But these studies represent a cross-section of the nation. Hardly a penetrating analysis of that very select group—those men and women who give major gifts, gifts over $1 million. How does this group feel about the tax implication of their giving?

Edwin Whitehead explains that when he first considered the idea of establishing a research institute, his attorney explained to him the tax consequences of a large gift and how it would actually enhance his estate. The idea of using the government's money to do something for mankind is what actually got the Institute started. But Whitehead says, "As you get into a project, the question of tax becomes less of a factor. I give at least the maximum I can get a tax advantage for, but I have long since exceeded that limit each year. The tax is no longer a motivating force for me. It's secondary after a long list of other important factors."

When Dmitri George made his million dollar gift recently to a hospital, the tax implication was not a factor at all. His father had received excellent care following a difficult and successful operation. Mr. George made the gift to show his appreciation. Dortch Oldham feels that the tax effect is not an important one in developing a gift. "If the government picks up some of the costs, that's fine. I take full advantage of everything I can. But I am positive that if there was not a tax incentive, I'd give the same amount."

Every major donor takes the fullest advantage possible of the tax dollar the government provides. It is doubtful, however, that this changes appreciably the philanthropic pattern of the major donor. Donors give, tax implication or not. The fact that the government participates in the giving allows the donor to do even more. George Pardee fits this category.

"There are several things which affect my giving in a major way. The tax consideration is always a factor, but I find that that is not the first thing I think about. From a tax standpoint, I usually come out about right at the end of the year, but it is never an overriding concern in my giving. It's not because of the tax situation that we make our gifts, but it does enable us to be as generous as we are."

Louise M. Davies has a banker and an attorney who work with her in her tax planning. She listens to them, but still does as she chooses. "Tax is certainly not a factor with me. It really isn't. I have a young attorney and a young banker and they try to give me guidance. Sometimes they say things like, 'Now, maybe you ought to think a little more before putting all of that money into that program.' I always listen to them, but I do what I want. I always make the gift first, and then we worry about the tax. I'm just about always beyond getting any sort of a tax advantage."

For some, the tax laws provide a general, but not prescriptive, guideline. Leo Beranek says that taxes are important to him although they have never been an overriding factor. They help establish the amount he gives. For years, he has been setting aside about 15 per cent of his income for philanthropy. The major benefit for almost all donors is the great personal satisfaction, not the tax advantage. Cyril Magnin says, "I don't give very much thought to the tax consideration. I get paid off in the satisfaction of knowing that I am doing something that is good. That's a great payoff. I don't consider the tax at all when making a gift. Especially in today's situation. It simply is not a factor. It is not important." James Gamble disregards the tax consideration entirely. "I suppose I should pay more attention to it, but it isn't part of my thought process at all when I make a gift. I know that I am way beyond the limit allowed by the law anyway." Virginia Piper agrees. "Tax benefits of giving just don't seem to mean anything to me. I give consideration to it, of course, but it's not the major force behind my giving. It is fair to say that I really don't give it a thought."

Almost all of the major donors give a great deal of money for what they consider to be worthy endeavors and for which there is no tax consideration. This helps confirm the thesis that the tax consequence is not of priority concern.

Leo Roon, for instance, showed me a letter he had just received from a paraplegic. Mr. Roon had been supplying scholarship assistance and medical care to him for years. Tax was never an issue—he did it out of an immense feeling of satisfaction. The same story could be repeated in the case of every major donor. Friends who need help, scholarship assistance, a small personal gift to a needy friend, a vacation gift for their minister's holiday. The joy runs deep. Tax is not a question.

W. Clement Stone is another major donor who gives to worthy individuals, programs, and special family situations where the tax issue is not a consideration. It is clear that the tax advantage is of value, but almost never an overriding provocation. Stone says, "I don't give my gifts because of the taxes. But if it weren't for the tax consideration, I might not be able to give as much as I do. I go over the limit every year." Marianne Mori says that the taxes play a small role, of no concern at all. Homer Watkins is scrupulous about keeping accurate records and taking the full deduction possible. But he says that it has scarcely any impact on his giving and that he is beyond the limit each year. Virtually all the major donors say they would give about the same, whether there was a tax advantage or not.

"Do I give because of the tax benefits?" comments Alex Spanos. "That's ridiculous. Actually, I take advantage of everything I can, but that's not the important thing for me. I really never think about it at all."

Leo Roon estimates that he has given somewhere between $5 to $7 million since his retirement. But there is a great deal more that has not gone to tax-deductible charities. "I think a person who really enjoys giving doesn't worry so much about the taxes. I like to make sure my money goes for scholarship assistance for people I care about or to help a family that is in need. I consider that sort of thing as important as giving to an institution. There was a young boy, a cerebral palsy victim, who was a great friend of my grandson's. I knew that he was going to have a terrible time in life and so I decided to establish a trust for him. It amounts to about $100,000. Well, I'll tell you, that gives me just about as much satisfaction as any gift I have ever made. I believe that the ingredient you will find with all major donors is the sheer joy you get out of doing something for others.

"When I see a need that's important, we give. We give to a number of different causes. You'd be surprised at the variety, but it is always something that we care deeply about. Oh, once in a while we will give something because a friend solicits us—but that's always a small amount. The tax consideration is not a major factor ever. I declare everything I can, but it's not the major issue. I most often give more than I am allowed by law, and I've done it for years."

Virginia Piper's husband was a most generous giver. She feels she has learned a great deal from him about giving. "When my husband died, I realized for the first time the scope of his giving. And it was not only to special causes and institutions. A lot of it went for needy families and people he felt showed great promise. I do that myself now a good bit. I am sponsoring a young man in medical school right now. He has tremendous potential and I have great faith in him. I do this in a quiet way and I really don't care for any recognition for it. It's just something I feel I should do. And of course, I don't receive any tax benefit for it." Dorothy Simmerly is another with the same motivation. "I give to a lot of people who are in need. A lot of people who need my help. There's no tax consideration at all. I just love to give to those where I can be of help."

Most of the major donors give beyond the maximum limit. Dorothy Simmerly considers the tax factor in her giving but points out that generally it doesn't do any good. She gives far beyond the limit. She says she gives because she wants to. Arthur Rubloff is another who goes beyond the amount allowed by law. ''I disregard the tax question completely. It has no relevancy in my determining whether I would make a gift or not.''

Several of the staff of The Urban Institute predicted a loss of $18.3 billion in individual contributions over the next four years due to the effects of the Tax Reform Act of 1981. It was a chilling forecast. And totally inaccurate. Philanthropy increases each year. A larger amount than the year before. This, in spite of recessions, difficult years, economic vicissitudes, and five major revisions of the Tax Law. The plain fact is that people give more in difficult times. This is especially true of the major donors. They give greater amounts. And the tax advantage is only an incentive, nothing more. The major donors most often give beyond the allowable amount.

In difficult economic times, the tax implications notwithstanding, major donors will tend to do even more for their special programs. Make sacrificial gifts. At times, even invade their corpus in order to do something significant. The key here, however, follows the pattern I have suggested. Major donors will tend to give large gifts to those organizations they have supported in the past. Especially in difficult times, the chances of a large gift going to a previously unfunded organization is minimal. Further, the more successful organizations will raise more money. Those in dire plight will have a more difficult time.

In interview after interview, I was told that the tax consequence of a gift was not the overriding factor.

Most donors do not even consider it. Do I take that at face value? I do!

By training, I am a listener. In a major way, that is how I make my living. Listening. Before I started the interviewing, I had an opportunity to read the two Gallup studies, both indicating that the tax advantage was little understood and not a major concern in giving. But that was with a cross-section of the nation, the large givers as well as the small. I was ready to talk with million dollar givers, and this was an issue I wished to probe persistently and intensely.

With each million dollar donor, we talked about the tax question. I explored. Scrutinized. Poked and examined. I inquired in a variety of ways. I do not feel I am naive. I am convinced that the responses were open, direct, and candid. And from the heart.

The Gallup Poll studies confirm what I discovered. The generous giving to individuals where there would be no tax advantage confirms what I found. On top of all of that, most of the group I interviewed were friends, and if not friends at least men or women I felt I knew well. They had nothing to prove, not to me, not to anyone.

I am convinced that with those I spoke with, the response was from their heart-of-hearts. They take as full advantage as possible of the tax incentives. Why shouldn't they? But in the case of each one, this was not a motivating factor and many give far beyond the limit provided under law.

Is this therefore true of every donor? Of course not! I have seen too many cases where a prospective donor and his accountant sharpen their pencil to a razor point before making a gift. I feel, however, the evidence is clear. You do not sell a major donor by talking about the tax advantages. That is not a compelling factor. And for many, it is not a factor at all.

*   *   *   *   *

Those organizations which are currently in desperate straits because they depended so heavily on governmental financing will not raise money because their need from the private sector is now more urgent and greater. They will only raise major funds because they offer donors rewarding satisfaction and exciting opportunity. Opportunity and dire need are not necessarily inclusive.

All major donors expressed in one way or another a certain pleasure in knowing that the government is sharing in their personal gift. Robert Saligman says that it certainly helps his giving to know that the government shares in what he does. Edwin Whitehead has a pet theory he expounds, often without being asked! He has a formula he would apply to corporate giving which he feels could measurably increase the amount that corporations could provide philanthropy.

Whitehead says that under today's tax rulings, ''There is no incentive for corporate donations because corporate investment for profit has the identical tax treatment as a corporate philanthropic donation. If corporations are allowed a direct tax credit for philanthropic causes, I believe most corporations would opt to make such donations.'' ''In other words,'' he points out—growing with enthusiasm for his plan, ''the business of business would not be affected, but all of the non-profits would benefit enormously.'' Do others agree with the plan and feel it has merit? He laughs. "I'm a patient man. (He isn't at all!) Little by little, I'll sell the idea. It could make a substantial difference in what corporations give away. And it makes so much sense."

There was a time when major donors greatly resented what they considered to be government interference in their favorite charities. I can still remember a board meeting I attended at Berea College in Kentucky. The directors were absolutely adamant. They would accept no federal funding. The college must depend on the private sector. Generally, that attitude has long passed. There are still some institutions which are hold-outs, they will not accept any government support, but they are few. Wheaton College in Illinois, Loma Linda University in California, Oral Roberts University—almost all institutions with a religious orientation, and almost all evangelical. Most institutions continue to seek government support with a certain fervor. With the major reduction that is now underway, there's a downright scramble for federal funds.

At one time, there was paranoia about accepting government funds. Too much interference. Too much intrusion. It is also possibly true that an organization's major donors and probably most of its board members were men and women of a more conservative persuasion. Politically conservative. "Do for yourself," that would have been the order of the day.

It is generally conceded now that the human and social problems which infest this nation cannot be solved by the private sector alone. It is a case of "there is so much to be done and so little money to do it." One university president with a particularly heavy emphasis on federal funding for his research programs faced the government cut-backs with concern and trepidation. He said he felt like he was all alone, in a small rowboat, in the middle of the ocean.

Foster McGaw, for one, feels strongly that it is of crucial importance for individuals to provide private support for institutions. He is convinced that the government will in time destroy the American way of life. Not all major donors share this sort of phobia, but almost all indicate they feel that gifts from the private sector are more cost-effective, are most flexible, and are faster to move into the mainstream of the institution's program needs. Less prone to meddling. Rigidity. Regulations. Red tape.

Among those who give, especially donors, there is clear evidence of a definite pride in giving from the private sector. Amon Carter, Jr. says "As far as I am concerned, I'd like to get the government out of all our organizations and universities. The less they are involved, the better it will be."

But donors need no inducement. They are already giving. What about the non-donors? For every million dollar donor, there are dozens with comparable resources who do not give. The private sector philosophy is not an argument for them, one way or the other.

14
THOSE WHO GIVE—GET

According to the Calvinist reformers, charity is "lending to the Lord, who in good time will return the gift with increase."

I KEPT CHECKING the address and the map as I drove to his office in Los Angeles. At best, this could be called a neighborhood in transition. There had been a recent influx of Mexican immigrants. Security guards stood at the doors of his headquarters, which was equipped with buzzers and one-way mirrors. A security guard accompanied me to his office, not a very fancy one for a man who has done so well.

Gerald Jennings heads Jennings & Cummings, manufacturers of wheelchairs. The Cadillac of the field, and the largest selling. Jennings was one of the early ones in the business, possibly the first. He took a baby carriage and converted it into a wheelchair. Crude, but a lifesaver.

In a sense, he is now all alone, he and his wife. They had hoped their son would assume the responsibilities for the company, but as it turned out he was not interested in the business. Jennings continues to head the corporation.

"It's a bewildering thing," he says to me. "When I first started in this business, we weren't making any money. We were just scratching out a living." There wasn't much at all, as he tells it, but his wife and he decided they would give away 10 per cent of all they earned, meager as it was.

It was just about at that time, when the decision was made to tithe, that the business began to change. And the more it prospered, the more Jerry Jennings and his wife gave away. They gave it away as fast as it came in.

There finally came a period when they were doing so well, there was barely time to give it all away. "We really had to work," Jennings tells it, "to find the time to give it away thoughtfully and carefully." Then Jennings and his wife decided to be double tithers. Twenty per cent of their income. "The more we gave," he told me, "the more we earned. We have to work at virtually full speed now just to keep up with our giving. And frankly, we're afraid to stop. The Lord has been so good to us since we started giving."

There is something bewildering about tithing. Mystiyfing, even forgetting the biblical admonitions, it appears true—life is like a wheel, what you give comes right back to you.

Cotton Mather lived during the colonial era of this country and was one of its great philanthropists. He was instrumental in the founding of Yale University. He felt that philanthropy was a matter of repaying God for the obligation that was owed. But he was also absolutely convinced that "those who devote themselves to good devices usually find a wonderful increase of their own opportunities."

Is it really possible? Can a case be made for philanthropy? I mean, can it possibly be true that the more you give to charity the more you receive in return? I don't mean personal joy or inner satisfaction. I am speaking of a direct monetary return.

O. V. Blumenstiel is an attorney in Alliance, Ohio. I was quite young in the business when he told me this story, but I remember it well. He said that he really couldn't explain it. He wasn't certain he even wanted to try to explain it.

He told me how his church, the First Presbyterian in Alliance, brought a small group of the leadership together to talk about tithing. Vic says that they were told that if they tithed, they would be repaid many times over. That what they gave would be given back to them. Would be returned in multiples.

He was certain, Vic told me, his minister was talking about the great satisfaction we would have in knowing about the good we had done. "But a strange thing has happened. I hate to even talk about it. I found that my tithing had an almost direct relationship to my law practice and what I received."

The more dollars he gave to charity, the greater his income. Vic says that he had the satisfaction and inner joy of giving, but along with it he also earned more. From that small group in the church who first met to hear about tithing, several did decide to make the commitment. And their experience was virtually a repetition of O. V. Blumenstiel's.

I have heard from many others. The same experience. I do not suggest, not at all, that you tithe so that you can earn more. Obviously, that would be the wrong reason. Grossly improper. But for some, perhaps that's reason sufficient.

Dortch Oldham made a decision to tithe before he graduated from college. He was working his way through school, supporting himself entirely. But a portion of his small earnings went regularly to the church. He told me how he had virtually nothing, but no matter what he earned, a mite went to his charity. He had kept it up to this time and he tells me that the more he gives, the more he seems to have.

Marianne Mori is wealthy, the beneficiary of a large estate. She says, ''The more I give, the more I get. I know that sounds spooky, but it's true. When I give, the money seems to come back to me many times over. And the personal satisfaction is indescribable.''

Frederick T. Gates was a man of the cloth. He left the Baptist ministry and went into business. He became John D. Rockefeller's closest advisor.

Gates found it unbelievable. The faster JDR gave his money away, the more he seemed to earn. There appeared to be no end in sight, no time to relax. He had to give it away, faster and faster.

Gates, one day, admonished him. ''Your fortune is rolling up, rolling up like an avalanche. You must keep up with it. You must distribute it faster than it grows. If you do not, it will crush you, your children and your children's children!''

We were alone in his office, Alex Spanos and I. He looked around the room as if to make certain that no one else was listening. Quietly, he spoke. ''The more I give, the more I make. I can't explain it, but I know it's true. The more I give, the better I seem to do. I am absolutely convinced of it. I don't give for that reason, of course. But it definitely seems to work out that way. It did from the very beginning when I really started to give. It always has.''

There is a lesson here for fund raisers. But I don't know what it is or quite how to explain it. I know that we don't speak enough about the gospel of giving. How can we let people know that there is a direct return on their investment to charity? But at the same time, not relate philanthropy and charity on a monetary basis.

''I am absolutely certain, convinced,'' reports Clement Stone. ''The more I give away, the more I seem to receive in return.'' And Stone, he has given away millions.

15

THE JOY OF GIVING

"God loveth a cheerful giver."
—St. Paul
In his Second Letter to
the Congregation at Corinth

PERHAPS THE BEST has been saved for last.

The question was never really asked. Yet, it was a persistent theme which dominated nearly every interview. Every single major donor. It dealt with the joy of giving, the sheer ecstasy.

With each person, as I reviewed with them the factors that motivated their giving, a recurring subject was the inner satisfaction they received. I never initiated this aspect of the discussion. The comments flowed freely from each individual.

Louise M. Davies talks to me about the joy of her

giving. "When Ralph and I first started out, he was earning about three hundred dollars a month. Even then, he was giving to special projects. When Ralph died, the janitor from the building walked up to me and held my hand. He said, 'Mr. Davies put all of my seven children through school and college. Without him, it couldn't have happened.' I had absolutely no idea that Ralph had done this. As time went on, I found out about more and more small things that he had done. I think he gave for the sheer joy of giving. I know I do.

"I get a tremendous amount of joy out of my giving. To me, in many ways, that's the real payoff. It is a great satisfaction. It does something to you and for you, almost indescribable. It's a great feeling. Sometimes I think I don't deserve to feel as good as I do about my gifts. After all, my husband made it all and did it all. But in giving it away, the joy is all mine. I feel so good about it that it makes me somewhat humble.

"Making the gifts has done an awful lot for me. To get involved, it really does something for you. It makes you glow. That's the only way I can describe it. I glow! I feel terribly sorry for those who do not give. I think that each time we make a gift in some measure we are saying thank you for the gift of life. I think you give for the sheer joy and love of it. I know I do. And for the special glow you get in your heart. Since I started giving, a whole new world has opened up for me. I have discovered generous, kind, loving, wonderful people out there. People who give their time, their knowledge, their enthusiasm in helping, sharing and responding to their fellow men."

Leo Beranek isn't certain he would describe it precisely as joy. "What I feel in my giving is a tremendous satisfaction, a thorough delight in knowing that I am able to help others. It is my repayment to society for all that I have received."

Cyril Magnin is a joyful giver. "I am a grateful giver, a joyful giver. I love to give. I return a very good portion of what I have. I feel I give a great deal in relation to what I have. I don't want to leave anything. I want to give it away before I die. It gives me great joy and satisfaction. I want to be here to see people enjoy it. That means a great deal to me."

Giving does something almost indescribable for the donor. Robert M. Cunningham tells the story of William Black, chairman of the coffeehouse chain Chock Full O' Nuts. Black has given away millions to New York medical schools and hospitals. He describes the feeling eloquently. "Wouldn't you be thrilled to feel financially responsible, partly or wholly, for a major breakthrough in the field against a dread disease? I am thrilled to see my name inscribed in a plaque at the Columbia University Medical Research Center. Who wouldn't be? Doesn't the author feel joy in seeing his book in the bookstore window? Doesn't the artist sign his painting out of a feeling of accomplishment? I, too, am quietly happy and deeply grateful that I have been and am able to contribute something to society."

The joy of giving. That is perhaps what philanthropy is all about. The joy of giving. This may be the key.

It has been my experience, confirmed by every single interview I conducted, that there is a satisfaction to giving which knows no bounds. Giving, for the sheer joy of it. By and large, it is not done to challenge others, to inspire others, to motivate. These are factors, all important but peripheral. Joy, that is the inner motivation. The gifts are not made to meet averages or percentages. Nor to fit a gift table. For the sheer joy of it, that's what motivates giving.

James Gamble speaks about the satisfaction his philanthropy provides him. "Giving makes me feel great. My God, yes, it makes me feel absolutely great. There's much gratification in making a gift, and maybe that's part of the ego involved. I believe that this is true of every major donor."

Alex Spanos explains it by saying that there is a special feeling, you're able to do something others can't do. "That's important. That really sets you apart. I'm really grateful that I'm in a position to give. It's partly ego but I get a tremendous kick, a great joy and satisfaction out of my giving. I feel lucky that I can do it. Fortunate that I am making enough money to do it. And I like the feeling of knowing I can do it. And I love the joy I get out of doing it."

The widow of Russell Sage, at his death, gave his fortune to start a foundation. The result was electric. "I am nearly eighty years old," Mrs. Sage said, "and I feel as if I were just beginning to live." Virginia Piper relates her feeling. "I love to give. Anyone would enjoy giving. I feel it's an honor to be able to, to be in a position to give. In a sense, I feel these are funds which are turned over to my care as a gift, which I must pass on to others. It is an awesome responsibility and I do the very best I can. And I love to be in a position to give. It is something that provides me my greatest joy in life."

George Peabody was a great American philanthropist. He provided major gifts for countless worthy causes in the States as well as in England. He spoke often of the great joy he felt in giving—much more, he said, than he deserved. It was following a conversation with Peabody, who spoke about the sheer joy and pleasure of giving money away, that Johns Hopkins decided to leave $7 million in his will for a university and hospital.

Annabelle and Bernard Fishman, of Philadelphia, give for the sheer joy of it. For their twenty-fifth wedding anniversary, they decided to build a school in Jerusalem. There was no direct connection, no ties to the children or the school principal. The Fishmans just felt that it would be a fun thing to do. And tremendously important, also. When the school was dedicated, the Fishmans went to Jerusalem with their family for the ceremony. It was a touching and an inspiring experience. And a tremendous moment of joy for all.

Arthur Rubloff says that when he makes a gift, he feels he is making a contribution to society. And that is what is important. "I get a kick out of that. It gives me great joy. It always has."

Not often in a person's lifetime is there an opportunity to do something significant, something really consequential. Something of lasting value. Giving to a really great cause is not a duty. It is a joy. We very seldom sell the joy.

Dorothy Simmerly understands the joy. She says: "When I make a gift, I feel good all over. I actually glow. I love to give. I patently enjoy giving. When you've got it, you're supposed to give it away. This is something I just feel inside me. And when I give, I look in the mirror and I think—wow, what a great thing I've done.''

W. K. Kellogg, the cereal magnate who provided funds for the Kellogg Foundation, protested that his giving involved no sacrifice. ''I love to do things for children because I get a kick out of it. Therefore, I am a selfish person and no philanthropist.''

George Pardee enjoys most of all making his gifts while he is alive to see the benefits. ''I get a really great satisfaction out of my giving while I'm alive. I don't really care about donations from my estate. I want to see things happen while I'm alive. I really enjoy giving. It's a great motivating factor for me. The sheer joy of being able to do something good. I really enjoy it. The truth of the matter is that I'm terribly happy to be in a position where I can make large gifts. I think people who are generous givers tend to be happy people. Part of that comes from the fact that it's so much fun to be able to give.''

There really is something to that. I have thought a lot about George Pardee's comment that givers are happy people. Among those I interviewed, there appeared to be an inner glow, a sense of great happiness. You could feel it. You could almost touch it. This has been true also, throughout my experience in the field. It is a gross generalization to say so, but I find that most major donors are happy people. Pleased with themselves. Their station in life. Happy to be in a position to be making a gift. Cheerful, positive people, each one of them.

For some, making a gift of real consequence to an institution may be like ''hitting the wall'' in a marathon.

It is painful at first, then it begins feeling good. It begins feeling very good. It's euphoric. My God, I've done it!

In my discussion with her, Marianne Mori said that she had thought a great deal about her giving and tried her best to discover the real motivation. "I often give because I want love from other people. I don't think that that is necessarily bad. It's a very human instinct. I feel that if donors were really introspective and thought about it, they would agree that this is often the reason for their giving. It's interesting and perhaps helps explain my point. It happens that I support two different churches quite heavily. I can actually feel the love that comes from this giving. I love helping people and I find great satisfaction in the love which is returned to me. There is the glow. The excitement. I love giving. It's almost neurotic."

Leo Roon says that it's the joy. The pleasure. He needs to see that his gift is going to be used for some important, general good. What gives him his greatest satisfaction is in seeing the money being put to good use. Edwin Whitehead claims that it's not an ego trip. "I just have great fun and enjoy seeing the results." Dmitri George says, "It's a feeling of accomplishment, to be able to make a gift. The sharing. The opportunity to give."

W. Clement Stone talks to me about the exhilaration he feels in making a gift. "I walk over to my desk, take out my pen, and get ready to sign a check for an important program. It's a great thrill. It means that I've done something that is very important. There's great joy in my giving. It's thrilling. It's exhilarating. It's important to be a part of sharing. It is my love. It is my joy."

Those who give find it rewarding and fulfilling beyond measure. There is an electrifying joy. A tremendous exhilaration. There is, by the way, a direct relationship between this, the joy of the donor, and those who work for institutions in raising funds. The fund raisers— they love their institutions and they love their work. It seems to show. Those who get the greatest joy seem to do the best. This appears to be the common denominator which separates the great fund raiser from the so-so. A professional, yes. A strategist, yes. A tireless worker, of course. But those who are the best and the most effective —they feel the tantalizing and tingling joy. Every bit as much as the donor.

The effective fund raisers, they pulsate with joy. And another quality they seem to have in common—the really good ones—is creativity. William Moyers recently made a thorough study of creativity. He discovered that creative people are willing to take risks, have a strong sense of self, are driven to prove their worth, and are disciplined. The great fund raisers exhibit all of these qualities. Never bored. Excited about the work and mission. Great strategists. The drone, the drudger, the fund raiser immersed in the details and mechanics of the job will probably never raise mega gifts.

We spend a great deal of time convincing people of the needs of the program, The importance of the project. The mission of the institution. A great deal of time, and a great deal of money. Why don't we spend more time demonstrating to people how absolutely euphoric they will feel after they have made a gift to the program. Why don't we do a more effective job of selling the joy?

The exhilaration? The inner glow? It is perhaps what philanthropy is all about. The love and joy of giving.

*   *   *   *   *

There are two other factors which are peripheral, for some even subliminal. But they are to be reckoned with. There is the great joy. There is also an unrelenting drive to repay, to make good. A sense that life has been better to these major donors than they perhaps really deserve. And philanthropy is their most direct way of repaying the debt.

Many also spoke about the great satisfaction they felt in being in a position to give. Life is good to them. They have done well. This is their way of saying thank you. When we speak to people about consequential giving we need to find a way of helping them show their gratefulness. It is unquestionably a factor in their giving.

Arthur Rubloff says, "I get great satisfaction out of making a gift. A tremendous indescribable joy. That's it—it's the joy of it. It's the whole idea behind my philanthropy."

And that, that is what philanthropy is all about!

16
TENETS FOR SUCCESS

*"He who is inclined to making many pronounce-
ments and practicing profundity, is in grave danger of being compared to the blacksmith's
bellows—providing great bursts of hot air under
pressure, but having not spark nor fire in itself."*
—John Russell

WHAT DOES IT all mean? I spoke with more than thirty
men and women who recently made gifts of over $1
million. I collected data from over 1000 field-tested
professionals in the fund raising field. As for me, I bring
nearly forty years in this magnificent business of helping
others undertake consequential acts of kindness and generosity.

There are clearly factors and forces which motivate
large gifts. What have I discovered?

I know full well the danger of proffering great pro-
nouncements. To many, fund raising is more an art than

a science. Each major gift most likely represents the convergence of a variety of stimuli and inspirational impulses, all of which are probably impacted by the serendipity of the moment. It would be easy to believe that causation and the human elements are so confoundedly intertwined that it is impossible to cast a guide, a pinpoint accurate focus on the elements of motivation. Not true.

I found a common thread woven throughout the fabric. A well-defined, unbreakable thread which links almost all the large giving.

Those who wish to argue the point may say that any list, no matter how clairvoyant would, by the very nature of the human mystery, be too sweeping in nature to be helpful. The disclaimers will say that since no two people are alike, the opportunity and the temptation to generalize are great. Like the blacksmith's bellows of John Russell, great bursts of hot air under pressure but devoid of spark and fire. Not true.

What I offer here is my own personal experience. This has now been greatly tempered and molded by those I interviewed who actually made the large gifts. My attitude has been further fashioned by the 1000 replies I received from hardened professionals in the field. The sheer weight of their feelings has to be considered heavily.

What emerges from all this is a clear theme. I am unshakably confident that there are clarion and distinct signs. Even glaring generalizations will be accurate most of the time. Some axioms of such profound good and common sense, they demand repeating—no matter how basic and fundamental they may seem. The proof is irrefutably conclusive. There is more commonality in the factors which motivate giving than there are differences. And as extraordinarily unique as people are, the drive and consideration which propels them to a major gift is very much the same.

During the preparation of this book I combined all I heard and read. I mixed this generously and openly with my own feelings and attitudes. Some "truisms" I have held dear for years clung like barnacles. Fund raising verities, it turns out, are sometimes more hollow than hallow. What has evolved are sixty-five factors which I am convinced guide, shape, and determine the success of securing the mega gifts. There is undeniable evidence. Even the blacksmith's bellows give me no pause: I offer these without apology or agony. The sixty-five tenets will provide the road map, the signs and signals, which will direct you to securing major gifts for your institution. If I repeat myself on some of these, or come close to doing so—very well, I think those cases merit a double dose of attention.

THE TENETS

1. Do not say "no" for anyone.

Be bold and daring. Go after your top prospects with persistence and passion, and all the vigor and zeal you can muster. You will be hurt more by those who would have said "yes," but were not asked, than by those who say "no." Few commandments in fund raising are as sacrosanct as this. Note it well.

2. Giving by living men and women outstrips every other form of philanthropy.

Over 80¢ of every dollar is given by a living man or woman. This highlights the consequence of developing in your program a creatively conceived strategy for the weighing, wooing, and winning of your individual prospects. Obviously, keep in mind that corporate boards, and foundation executives and boards, consist of people with the same sort of human strengths and frailties which guide the giving of individuals. A foundation may have well defined roles which govern its giving, but even within these limitations, the foundation executive and board will make decisions with the same intuitions, perceptions, and hang-ups as individuals.

3. Individuals give emotionally, not cerebrally.

They do not give to needs. They give to dreams and dazzling visions. Giving is visceral. Individuals will view your long list of details and specifics with appropriate pious and quiet applause, but this will seldom move mega givers to audacious action. Columns of statistics, financial statements, and historical facts may be very important for substantiation and background. But large donors appear unmoved by such minutiae and tedium. No unrestrained exhilaration in this sort of stuff! And by the way, in several studies we have conducted recently with a large number of leadership people, we find that the majority of men and women cannot read blueprints. Further, virtually all of the group were unmoved and uninspired by blueprints and floor plans. We have been putting them in campaign folders for years. We have now stopped.

4. **The "Rule of Thirds" is a canon that has persisted since the earliest of fund raising programs.**
   It persists today, and, while there may be some exceptions, the Rule is virtually scriptual: 1/3 of your funds in a campaign program will come from your top ten to fifteen gifts; 1/3 will come from your next 100 to 125 gifts; the remaining 1/3 will come from all the other gifts. There is evidence now that in current campaigns for institutions where they have had a capital program in prior years, the requirement for larger gifts is even greater—there are fewer gifts, but those which are generated are at a much higher level. The base of the giving pyramid is less broad; the tip, more important than ever. Structure your campaign program on the need of securing your top ten to fifteen gifts to represent 1/3 of your campaign goal. You can count on it.

A corollary to this is that try as you may, you simply cannot win a campaign by arithmetic. It has been attempted often, and always with disastrous results. The project is moribund. A midwestern college needs to quickly raise $600,000 to finance a project. "That should be easy," says one enthusiastic alumnus. "We'll just get 600 of our graduates to give $1,000 each." Never! It simply won't work. The Rule of Thirds will persist—$200,000 will come from the top ten to fifteen gifts. The same Rule applies to a $6 million, or a $66 million program.

5. **Almost without exception, husbands and wives together will discuss their major philanthropy.**
   Virtually always, the husband and wife will confer before making a final commitment for a mega gift. Give serious thought, therefore, to initiating your discussion regarding the gift with both the husband and wife, even though only one partner may be particularly interested in your program. Otherwise, you run the risk of having the potentially teachable and interpretive discussion take place without your being present to run the interference, respond to questions, and overcome objections.

6. **Seek ways that you can involve both the husband and the wife in the program and activities of the institution, even though only one of the partners demonstrates an obvious interest.**
   Make certain that both receive credit and recognition, even though only one partner may have carried

the major responsibility for the gift. This lessens the possibility of divided loyalties. And it helps ensure a continued interest in your institution by the surviving spouse.

7. **I find no clear evidence that the spirit, passion, and dedication to philanthropy is passed on from one generation to the next.**
Countless unmistakable examples indicate this is the case; but you'll find just as many notable exceptions. If you go after the son or daughter for a gift because the parent was extremely generous, it is entirely possible that you will be on a misguided, misdirected mission. The new generation will want to give because of a mix of factors and the appeal of the program, and not because wealth has been handed down from one generation to the next.

8. **A mega gift comes from an individual who has the resources to make it. That states the obvious. In the case of many such donors, it is harder to get an appointment than it is to get the gift itself.**
More strategy, planning, and innovation may be required to get the appointment than will be required to sell the program. Use the best person and contact possible to make the appointments and open the door.

9. **A very good friend is quite often not the best person to make a solicitation—although he or she may be the best to make the appointment.**
Often, a friend will be overly protective and may

find it difficult to overcome a "I don't think so" attitude on the part of the potential donor. It will be much easier for a friend to switch to making a date next week for a golf match.

10. **In my experience, children are not effective in soliciting their parents for a major gift.**
Without question, they will be effective in securing gifts for a pet project, but never a mega gift. I have questioned a number of professionals in the field on this tenet, and I find no exceptions.

11. **Securing the mega gift means helping the major donor desire more than anything to share in your dream.**
The donor's design must fit your objective. The sooner your vision is shared and the transfer is made, the quicker the decision will be to make the gift. Successful fundraising is simply effective marketing. And effective marketing is helping others to meet their needs while accomplishing yours.

12. **The decision to give is spontaneous.**
There is almost an immediate spark of electricity. The amount may still be in doubt, the timing may be a question, the manner in which the gift will finally be made may require further study—but the decision is made. If a great deal of time is requested by the potential donor to make a decision or, if on subsequent visits, no definite move puts the gift into action, the odds are that you are not going to receive a mega gift.

13. **The commitment regarding the major gift will likely not be made on the first visit.**
    If it is, the chances are that you are not getting as much as you should. This being the case, spend most of your time during the first call selling the drama, the power, and the excitement of the program.

14. **The case for the gift must be stronger and bigger than the institution itself.**
    There must be a demonstration of a more significant platform. Find one and use it.

15. **Do not sell the needs of the institution.**
    Virtually all organizations and programs have needs. People do not give to needs, they give to opportunities. Bold, visionary, exhilarating opportunities. Individuals require their own needs to be met. Listen carefully. See how you can mold the needs of the potential donor to the opportunities of the proposed program. Mega givers will buy what they choose, not what you are trying to sell. The trick is in making certain that what they want most is what you want most.

When Robert Schuller decided that he needed to expand his church to meet a bulging membership of 8000, every addition and renovation the architect proposed met with a dull, uninspired ho-hum by the congregation. Then an excited Schuller said: "I want a totally new church, all glass. All glass!" Now that is an audacious opportunity. He inspired his congregation to make his dream theirs. What evolved is the Crystal Cathedral. All glass, star shaped, 414 feet from one point to the other. The glass roof is one hundred feet longer than a football field and seems to float in space. It soars twelve stories above the ground. The Crystal Cathedral is a daring venture, the result of the vision of those who made it their own dream.

16. Listen.

Help the prospect sell your program. Watch for the signals. Get the prospect as close to the program as possible. The best auto salesman gets you into the driver's seat. You feel the wheel. You look at the gleaming dashboard. For one glorious moment, you are speeding through the Italian Alps, over a twisting, turning road. For most people, reading the torque-ratios and compression factors may be interesting, but it's the driver's seat that gets them. Get your prospect behind a steering wheel. Walk the prospect through the campus, into the emergency room, remember what it was like to be nine years old and away at camp.

17. Listen!

18. Megagivers seem to be people filled with joy.

You can pick them out in a crowd. I haven't been able to really figure out why, but it's true—there's a dedicated and recognizable joy to their living—a *joie de vie*. It may be that they have reached that stage where they are able to make a large gift. That is reason enough for joy. It may be that because they make large gifts, they feel they are on the side of the angels. But there is the definite thrill and joy to living. I have no proof of this, but it seems to me that mega givers live beyond the actuarial tables. Gerontologists claim that people live longer when there is the will and the drive to live, and the joy of the moment, the hope for the future. Perhaps this is the connection.

You doubt me, I know it. But just think of those you know who are the really large givers. Note their age and their attitude. Then write me a letter of apology.

19. A person with no experience in giving will almost never make a major first gift.

Giving is a habit. The fact that a person has great resources provides no assurance at all that a gift will be made. How often have you heard: "That person has enough money that they could give the whole campaign goal." But they won't, not if they haven't had the experience and exhilaration of giving in the past. Make the call anyway. You can't win if you don't begin. Be satisfied with a smaller gift than you had hoped for. Show appreciation, cultivate, recognize. Call again for a gift. And again. Gradually, that smaller first gift will grow into a much larger one. Take to heart the words of Harold J. Seymour. The doyen of fund raising said: "You don't make a pickle by sprinkling a little vinegar over a cucumber. You have to soak it."

20. **Believe.**

Feel and think what it will be like to secure the mega gift. Engage the extraordinary power of the possible. Make a giant leap of faith. If you are fairly certain that you will probably not get a gift, the odds are you won't.

21. **Giving is emotional.**

A love affair. Even among those who work to be most calculating and thoughtful about their giving— it is most often the visceral which sets the fire. Both women and men tend to think that women are more emotional and less studied in their giving. Among the large donors, this is not true. The thrill and excitement is equal. The emotional sparks ignite the same flame in both.

22. **Major donors give their largest gift to those institutions where they serve on the board or in an official capacity of some sort.**

Interestingly, they often do not recognize that this is a factor in their giving. Perhaps the motivation is subtle. It is a plain fact, however, that familiarity begets involvement, and involvement begets commitment, and commitment begets giving. Often, sacrificial giving. The more people know about you and the more involved they are, the much more likely they are to be committed to your great aspirations and grand designs. Involvement provides a quantum escalation to a mega gift.

It does not necessarily follow that everyone on the board will make a sacrificial gift to the program. It does often follow, however, that your most sacrificial gifts do come from people on the board or those who have served in some official capacity in the past.

An institution will do well in assuring its future by giving serious consideration to the three "W's" that each trustee should bring to the board table: *W*ork, *W*isdom, and *W*ealth. Fortunate the institution that has directors who bring all three "W's." It's brilliant success and growth are assured. The organization with the one "W" directors will probably not survive in today's world.

23. **Dedicated, devoted board members are the lifeblood of an organization.**
The strong, effective, influential, and affluential men and women—the three "W" variety—are becoming increasingly more difficult to recruit. Your board profile provides one of the vital signs for the organization, an unshakable index of your ability to grow and develop. Potential board members who show promise and resolve should be pursued and romanced with all of the ardor and fervor you place in engineering a large gift. In many ways, the dedicated board member is even more important than the large gift. A board of dogged determination and dedication can accomplish any objective for your institution.

24. **A sense of duty and responsibility provokes the mega giver, but it is a factor which is difficult to interpret and describe.**

Many people have great resources and give nothing. Obviously, they subscribe to no feeling of duty or responsibility. Among those who make large gifts, they seem to consider it a willing, rewarding, and gratifying responsibility. No guilt is involved. Their giving is not related to a somber, solemn duty.

There is no end to the number of requests. One after another. An endless stream. In desperation, the man calls for an angel. The angel appears.

> "Angel, angel—how long must I
> keep giving?"
> The angel looked at the man—
> The glance pierced him through.
> "You may stop giving,
> when the Lord stops giving to you."

Among those who give, there is a real and felt presence of deep gratitude. Life has been strikingly good to them—for some, inexplicably and unaccountably so. There is the compulsion to repay somehow for this good fortune. It is not guilt. For some, it may even be a nod of voodoo to the supernatural. Just in case!

25. The staff leadership determines the character, the vitality, the growth, and the personality of an institution.
A dynamic institution is led by a dynamic staff. Propelled with the zeal of a dedicated missionary.

Mega givers respond to vigorous and inspirational staff leadership. It is one of the most compelling factors in motivating a gift. In all of my experience, I do not know of a really major gift that was made to an institution where the donor did not have high regard and respect for the Chief Executive Officer. No matter how dedicated the Christian is to his church, he will give even more if he has steadfast admiration for the minister. No matter how grateful a person is to the hospital, he will give an even greater amount if he has esteem for the staff. No matter how sentimental and indebted a man may feel about his alma mater, the gift will be even more sacrificial if there is affection and admiration for the President. I know of no situation to challenge this hypothesis. The consequential role that staff plays in motivating the mega gift is irrefutable.

26. The position of the staff is singularly dominant in influencing the mega gift.
It is persuasively important that the Chief Executive Officer be involved in some major manner in developing the strategy and actually making the call for a gift.

27. Chief Exective Officers who do well at fund raising enjoy it.
Some thrive on it. A few even lust for it. Those who do not do well, do not like it.

28. With regard to volunteers soliciting potential large donors, it is far better to have the #1 commitment of a lower level volunteer than the #2 or #3 commitment of the highest level volunteer.

The most influential person possibly will not be your most effective solicitor unless he or she brings an immovable, overwhelming, uncompromising committment to the program.

29. Women can be extremely effective fund raisers.

It is their fervor and dedication that will count. In some instances, however, they may need assistance in opening the door and making the appointment.

30. Determine with painstaking strategy who should make the call.

Generalizations are never valid—but, of course, this is only a generalization. Here are some walloping vague principles which is the price you pay for generalizing. It is difficult for a younger woman to solicit an older woman or widow. The latter is accustomed to dealing with older attorneys and accountants, most often her husband's and most often male. She is comfortable in this setting, much less so with the young female. Young, attractive women are not effective in soliciting large gifts from middle aged men.

Nuns are more effective when they wear their habit. Nuns are very effective calling on men and women. Priests are more effective calling on women. Father Wasson is one of the great fund raisers of the decade. He personally raises millions each year for his orphanage in Mexico. In Mexico, priests are not allowed to wear the clerical cloth outside the church. When Father Wasson comes to the States to raise money, he becomes "a man of the cloth" and dons the vestments we are familiar with in this country. That's smart fund raising!

Sons and daughters are not effective in securing major gifts from their parents. They can almost always get a small donation for a pet project in which they are interested. Don't send one of the children to make the call. Interestingly, a son-in-law can be much more effective. A parent can be extremely successful in soliciting one of the children.

31. **Mega givers experience a spiritual sensation in their giving.**

This does not necessarily have anything to do with the formal church or organized religion. But there is the tingle of righteousness, sometimes even close to piousness, in their giving. There is almost always a great deal of love and near reverence for the institution which is the beneficiary of the megagift. For many, when the major gift is made, there is a mystical soul-stirring which transcends the commonplace. It is an important factor in motivating the large giver. Not God-fearing, but godly. Generally, mega givers feel deeply about religious and spiritual matters. Many are ardent and faithful church goers, but some espouse what Robert Frost felt: "There is much of deeper spiritual meaning outside the Church than in."

32. **Never in the history of this nation has there been an era with greater priority and urgency for the delivery of human and social services.**

It is a time of clatter and clang. Emergencies and exigencies. Clamour and crunch. Many institutions in today's society will be unable to cope on this sort of a slippery and skimpy track. For countless, it's one minute 'til midnight. Even those who can manage will be stretched to the limit. The government's response has been to cut severely funding for human and social services.

The combination of the explosive precedence for services, balanced unevenly by these sobering reductions in federal and state funds, places an uncompromising burden on the private sector for financing. That's good news! As Clement Stone is so fond of saying: "You have a problem—that's great!' Problems represent swelling expectations and magnificent opportunities—just waiting for bold and daring institutions sufficiently venturesome to reach out. There has never been a more auspicious time or a greater receptiveness on the part of donors. For giving money to a great cause. A captivating, irresistible idea. There has never been a better time for your institution to raise money than now. There is no lack of money, only a lack of vision. It's there, all yours, for the asking.

33. Recognition of the donor is important—expressing appropriate appreciation, even more so.

Most mega givers indicate that they do not seek undue recognition. Overt honor and homage are not the required rewards for the donation. I believe that this is only partially true. I am convinced that appropriate recognition, tastefully and tactfully rendered—often with even a bit of elan—is welcome indeed and appreciated. Do not expect the donor to ask or seek this type of recognition. You must initiate the idea, encourage it, review it with the donor, enhance it until it is precisely to the point of providing the proper recognition for both your institution and the donor. The dividends for the careful planning and development of such a gift will be immense. And it initiates the first step in securing another and larger gift.

34. Quite often, a donor does not wish personal aggrandizement for making a mega gift.
Still, it is extremely important to your institution that recognition be given for the gift. It paves the way for gifts to follow. Suggest a way to honor the donor's family, a loved one, or a tribute to someone he or she greatly admires.

35. Practice the "Rule of Sevens."
Find a way to thank a person seven ways for their gift. I don't believe in formula-guaranteed answers to fund raising. But this one really works. The results will astound you.

36. Asking for a gift during lunch or dinner is not effective.

37. Large donors tend to stay with programs and activities that have been of interest over a long time.

They do not bounce back and forth from one institution to the other. If you are calling on a prospective donor, one who has been a major donor to other institutions but has not yet been generous to yours, the chances are quite slim that you will receive a mega gift for your program. But it is certainly well worth the attempt. Go after the prospect with all of the faith and hope you can marshal. Use the most powerful ammunition you can assemble. Almost certainly, you'll get a gift. It may not be as large as you had hoped for, but it will be a start. Build on that. Plenty of appreciation. Keep calling. Keep asking for new gifts. That's the road to a mega gift.

38. Exciting and daring programs sell.
Programs that are significant and can make a difference. Bold, but not controversial. Controversial and radical programs are extremely difficult to sell—no matter how great the urgency and need.

39. Those who will give to you in the future are men and women who have given to you in the past.
Your best prospects for a gift are those who have already given to you.

This tenet is flawless, even if a sizeable gift has just been made to your institution. Say, for instance, that you are very near the completion of your campaign—the bottom half of the ninth inning!—but you still haven't reached your goal. You evaluate the prospects who still have not committed themselves to the program, and even if the appraisal looks promising, it doesn't appear that you'll be able to reach your goal. What to do? Call on those who have already given to the campaign—but haven't done as much as they could have or you expected? No! Don't call on them. Call on those who have already made a very large and generous gift. They will do more. And they will be pleased that you asked.

40. **Men and women are much less likely to give to an institution—no matter how exciting and tantalizing the new project might be—if it has problems with its annual operations.**
Financial stability of the institution is considered one of the prime requisites of the donor. There is little comfort in making a mega gift unless there is assurance and confidence that the organization has had a sound fiscal operation in the past and shows financial stability for the future. This need not be the major emphasis in a presentation—after all, this is not selling "the sizzle." On the other hand, proper fiduciary responsibility and stewardship do need to be stressed.

41. **People do not give out of a sense or feeling of guilt.**
They do not give "till it hurts"—they give because it feels so good.

42. **Ego plays an important part in making a mega gift.**

Describing an emotional feeling can be, at best, imprecise. Most of the men and women who make large gifts concede that there is a tremendous amount of ego involved in their philanthropy. The recognition, the status it provides, the acclaim, and for some the permanent memorializing of their name. Even among those who protest vehemently any narcissistic factor to their philanthropy, I find a certain degree of self-serving indulgence. Not necessarily bluster, vain adulation, or aggrandizement. Still, an unquestionnable self-satisfaction and self-regard. I suggest you play for the ego. If in doubt, go for the ego. Even under protest, tickle the ego! It is a human quality, not without merit.

43. **A compelling, driving belief in the organization is singularly important.**
A love of the organization takes precedence over local pride and community spirit. Mega gifts are indeed made because the donor feels that the program will be good for the community, but overriding that issue is a passion for the organization. First sell the institution, then interpret how the program can be of everlasting benefit to the community, or to the world, or to mankind.

44. **Donors wish to give to something that makes a difference, a cause of consequential proportions, a program that has the potential for creating a significant change for good.**
Before making the call on the potential donor, review carefully your presentation. Determine how

the project can be developed into one which creates substantial, innovative, positive evolution. Even a new roof or the replacement of a boiler should be transformed into a selling point of significance. It must be for more than just filling a need. Odds of getting a mega gift are far better if the new roof can be shown to be a reordering of social and human services. The new roof is the steak; serving mankind is the sizzle.

45. Take nothing for granted.
Even members of the official institutional family, your closest board members, may not be as aware as you assume of your activities, your services, and your outreach. You sit and wonder how someone who has served on your board for years may not be informed fully of all you are doing, may not yet tingle with the excitement of your program. Take my word for it, many do not. Even with those closest to you, take the time to tell the full drama of your story.

46. Donors are intrigued by the yeast, not the pabulum.
"Seed gifts" have great appeal. Show how their donation can multiply gifts from countless others. This demonstrates that their dollars generate additional dollars in geometric proportions.

47. Men and women give to institutions, programs, and campaigns that are successful.
Programs that are popular. Programs that are being

subscribed to by others. They race for the bandwagon. They disdain the losing cause, the unpopular program, the campaign that is faltering.

Success succeeds. The successful organization becomes more successful. Those who need help the most are likely to be overlooked. Dr. Samuel Johnson once asked Lord Chesterfield, ''Is not a Patron one who looks with unconcern on a man struggling for life in the water, and when he has reached ground, incumbers him with help?''

48. Mega gifts are almost certain to be repeated.

Your best and largest donors are those who have given to you in the past. And almost never will that be their largest gift or their last.

49. People resent overbearing solicitors who push to make the sale.

They resist pressure and find it acutely repugnant. The most effective solicitor listens—and then moves directly to make the potential donor's dream one in the same with that of the institution.

50. Who makes the call for a gift is of critical importance, but it does not have to be a peer.

Being a friend or a peer can be of notable importance in opening the door for an interview and being present for the solicitation. A friend may not, however, be the best person possible for interpreting the institution or asking for the gift. A friend calling on a friend, peer on peer (the old hoary fund raising verity), can often be a downright mistake.

51. **Experience shows that mega gifts are often given as a result of the Chief Executive Officer of an institution calling on a prospect.**
In case after case, there is undeniable proof that the C.E.O. is often the most important and effective person.

52. **Mega givers refer to one quality in particular which they feel is most important in the person making the call: *integrity*.**
They must respect the person and hold him or her in high regard and esteem. In some circumstances, it need not be the chief officer of the institution; it may be another staff person who is closely involved with the project or the potential donor.

53. **Matching the gift of others has little effect on securing mega givers.**
They will not aspire to a matching invitation. A Challenge Gift, on the other hand, can inspire a mega gift from a donor.

54. **For many, campaign literature has the same éclat as the sound of one hand clapping.**
Often, campaign material is a turn-off. And the fancier the material, the more objectionable it is. The majority of serious donors feel that campaign literature is not relevant and much prefer a strong and compelling verbal presentation, substantiated by simple written documentation of the program.

Campaign literature can help influence smaller and medium sized gifts. It can also help measurably to provide aid and comfort to the solicitor. But for the really large sized gifts, use a different approach. The truth of the matter is that often the sophisticated and elaborate brochure is prepared to indulge the client.

55. More than two people can make an effective call.
A fund raising tale, repeated so often it is now accepted as Grail, states that more than two people making the solicitation are overwhelming to the prospective donor. Not true! Take as many people as you need. No fewer, no more. Evaluate carefully in advance what will comprise the most forceful and potent team. For the really large potential gifts, this should almost always include the senior officer of the institution.

56. Research your prospect with finite care and painstaking attention.
No detail is too small. What might appear to be an insignificant bit of information can often open the door to the mega gift.

57. Give your case a cold and calculating examination.
It may not be your strongest case at all. It may not have drama and emotional appeal. It may not provide the sizzle. There have been many instances where a small twist, a seemingly unimportant change, has made all the difference. Take for in-

stance the campaign for the Restoration of the Presidential Yacht Potomac. Funds were required to restore the yacht. It was raised from the sea floor, rescued from the salt water by a miracle of engineering and cranes, and completely stripped. But the Potomac has little historic marine value. It was not the first of its kind or the only one of its kind. Its fascination and inspiration lies in the fact that during some of the most crucial years in the history of this nation, it was "the floating White House." It was where Franklin D. Roosevelt held many important meetings. It was the President's escape-hatch, a floating diversion. The restoration of the Yacht had little appeal. The case for the campaign focused on President Roosevelt and the historic magic of the presidency.

58. The mission of the organization is of primary, overriding, and paramount significance.

Nothing else is as important. Everything else pales in importance. No matter how appealing the specific program or project may seem, nothing is as powerful an incentive as an abiding and impelling belief in the mission of the institution. Don't discuss the program, the campaign, the need. First, sell the mission.

59. The more donors give, the more they seem to get back.

This is a fascinating, almost mystical, by-product to philanthropy. Givers receive in return many-fold what they give away. Giving is like a moving wheel. Gifts come back in major dividends. This cannot be explained, but it is recognized by major donors. It is not the reason they give, it is not the motivating factor, it is not the rationale. But the phenomenon does exist.

60. **Individuals tend to be less conforming in their bequests, and much more conservative in their giving while living.**
The majority of mega givers live prudent and conventional lives. They prefer a similar pattern for their philanthropy while they are alive.

61. **There is seldom a single, dominant reason for making a mega gift.**
It is most often the result of at least several motivating factors. Often, they are not even understood or recognized by the donor. And often they intersect and overlap. You will be most successful in securing the mega gift if you can determine in advance and during the call, the donor's motivation. Research and listen. Then, appeal to what you feel are the most stirring and provoking motivations.

62. **The mega giver takes every advantage under the law the government provides for philanthropy. At the same time, evidence proves—and I am convinced—that the tax advantage is not the primary force behind their giving.**
And for many, it is not a factor at all. Don't sell the tax advantage. Don't even assume that it will have an impact on their giving to your program. Place the

strength and power of your presentation on the mission of your institution.

63. **Every mega giver experiences an exhilaration and ecstasy in philanthropy.**
Joy in their giving knows no bounds. Find a way to sell the joy. John D. Rockerfeller said: "Long ago I lost the joy in living. The only joy I have is in my giving."

64. **Fund raisers must consistently and persistently seek out the potential mega giver.**
Fund raisers can be classified with what William James calls "the faithful fighters." It's what the Greeks called the Agon—the struggle, the match. It is also the derivative for the word agony. And there is certainly agony involved in the work. But fund raisers are an unusual lot. They love the battle and the struggle. Every day, they roll their rock up the hill. They enjoy the exhilaration of the fray. The strategy. The campaign. The winning. When the tardy and reluctant Crillon arrived too late for a great victory, Henry IV said: "Hang yourself, brave Crillon! We fought at Arques and you were not there." There are innumerable opportunities for mega givers to express their philanthropy. To be an effective fund raiser requires a certain quality of intrepidity, persistence, luck, and timing. For the fund raiser who has missed a mega gift to another institution: hang yourself, dear fund raiser—the precious moment existed, and you were not there. Next time, seize the opportunity.

65. Many tenets are important, but the greatest of these is: You must ask for the gift.

This may appear to be overly fundamental but too often, this cardinal principle is overlooked. This does not mean that you must necessarily ask for a specific amount—and as a matter of fact, in some situations this should be avoided. Many absolutely superb presentations are made where the interpretation and story of the institution are flawless, but where the solicitor finds it agonizing to ask for the gift. The tongue gets heavy and thick, the hands perspire. But every salesperson knows that finally, inevitably—you must ask for the order. This is the greatest commandment of all.

17
THE BEGINNING

"This is not the end. It is not even the beginning of the end. But it is, perhaps, the end of the beginning."

—Winston Churchill

LIFE THESE DAYS is frantic. A fast and slippery track. No one has even the time to read the introduction of a book. Not even a well written preface.

That is why the beginning of this book is at the end!

The president of Pluribus Press and I have talked for some time about the possibility of my writing a book on fund raising. The "for some time" is close to five or six years.

The long delay was not the result of any lack of interest. Our firm was going through a period of major expansion and development and there was sufficient work to keep me more than busy. Life was full. And the book itself took more time than I anticipated. The questionnaires and the tabulating of 1000 responses, the several dozen depth interviews, the drafting of the manuscript, the continual adding of material—revising and revising once more—then, just one last revision for spontaneity!

More than that, I really was not keen on writing another "how-to" book, a nuts and bolts of fund raising. There were already a number of these on library shelves. A few are excellent, many are pabulum. Harold Seymour's book, the *Fundamentals of Successful Fund Raising* (McGraw-Hill, 1951), remains a classic. No one will be able to improve on it. But Seymour's book deals mainly with campaign mechanics and procedures. I felt strongly that one of my great missions in life was to save the world from another book on campaign structure, how to organize a campaign office, how many prospects each worker should call on, how to recruit and train workers, and how to write a case statement that dazzles.

The publisher finally convinced me that what I have described is precisely what he did not want. He explained that his research had convinced him that the field really cries for a book on what motivates people to give. Really large gifts.

The more he talked, the more excited I got.

"I want to know why people really give. The whole field needs this kind of a book. What motivates them. I want the guts of it. I don't want a book on people. I don't want a book on campaign procedures. Skin away all the layers and get into the heart of it. Why do people make large gifts? What's the incentive? Right now, I think it's a mystery to everyone but if you are able to find the answer, I want to be able to tell the world."

What evolved has been an extraordinary experience for me and an unusual book. Perhaps the only one of its kind. With the publisher's unrelenting prodding, I attempted to get to the very heart of the question—what really motivates people to give.

The respected Gallup Organization conducted a study recently and asked the general public, "Why do you give to charity?" The overriding response was that the donor likes to help others. But that is hardly a penetrating answer, and may not be the answer at all. My quest was to a much more selective universe than Gallup's. I wanted to find out why people make mega gifts, gifts of $1 million or more.

Establishing the figure at $1 million for a gift was arbitrary. I suspect that it could have been fixed anywhere within the mid to high six figure category and the motivation behind the giving would have been about the same. On the other hand, there is something quite singular about a million dollar gift. The mid-six figure gifts are all special, and that's like taking it down to the two or three yard line. A million dollar gift somehow symbolizes taking it over the goal line. For me and for this book, the proper distinction was at $1 million or more. I am quite satisfied, however, that the same factors I uncovered at the million dollar level exist with most donors, large or small.

For this book, I spoke with over thirty men and women and interviewed twenty-two in depth. They were not chosen at random. For the most part they were friends, people I knew, people I have worked with in campaign programs. Not one really wanted to be interviewed and some did it only as a personal favor. By and large, these are very private people. Because they were mostly friends, I had the freedom to probe, inquire, speculate, imagine, and explore.

This is not the story of the people described in this book. Quite the contrary, most shied away from an interview, would much prefer to remain anonymous, and granted the interview mostly out of friendship. It is not their story. It is the story of giving.

Of the group, only three requested that their names not be used in the book. I have given each a pseudonym: Dmitri George, Dorothy Simmerly, and Homer Watkins. I have kept their description in the book sufficiently general so that they cannot be identified.

In addition, several thousand questionnaires were sent to fund raisers who are active in a variety of areas, mostly those with which I am familiar—hospitals and medical centers, educational institutions, YMCAs, cultural activities, and the Salvation Army. I was curious. What would their response be to the factors which motivate giving? After all, they are actually involved and are practicing the profession. How does their assessment compare with the men and women who actually made the $1 million gifts?

In selecting those for actual interviewing, I made no attempt to represent the population proportionately. Depth interviews were conducted throughout the country, but no attempt was made for pure geographical distribution. My approach was to try to develop a psychological portrait of the individual and his or her relationship to the institution and the gift. I felt that this would be far more significant and revealing than the colder, more clincal aspects of pure statistical data. And I frankly chose those with whom I could make an appointment easily—men and women I already knew. I interviewed men and women of all different ages and occupations. The focus was on a prepared form of factors but the responses and probing tended to be free-form and open-ended, following the lead of the interviewee. Consistent themes emerge and merge. For me, that is the most intriguing part of all. I use quotations heavily because they speak so vividly and pointedly to the issue. Dissecting the quotations, analyzing the variables point by point, would in some way destroy their essence—the human and intense quality, and the emotional impact of giving.

I make no case for the validity of my depth interviewing of twenty-two people. It could have been more, it could have been less. Indeed, it could have been a totally different group of twenty-two. In a recent article in *Town & Country* magazine, it was reported that last year there were twenty-one gifts of $1 million or more which were given to a variety of charities. Actually, the number is probably closer to thirty. These are gifts made by living individuals. In the preceding three years, there were twenty to thirty such donors. Many of the individuals mentioned in this article were those I actually interviewed. I feel certain that my group is valid for my purposes.

This book takes on great importance, perhaps greater now than ever before. These are grave times, complex times for you and your institution. You have many opportunities. A boundless number. There never a more exciting time to be in the business of raising funds.

I hope that book will challenge you to think smarter, work harder, plan bolder, commit yourself with fervor and missionary zeal to the needs of your institution. More than anything, I hope it provides you with a daring willingness to challenge, to explore, to break through old barriers. The rewards are great.

I am certain that history will deal kindly with you and your institution if you get into the fray, and throw your heart and passion into the excitement and delight of the unventured.

"Every major gift situation is a separate campaign, usually quite unlike the next," says Addison L. Winship II. These are difficult times, and the opportunities were never greater.

It is entirely possible that fund raising as an art is a passing phenomenon. It may have already seen its time of greatest glory. Soon we old time fund raisers will be turned out to pasture, to graze out our days dreaming of old ways and trying to remember what exactly they were all about. It is quickly becoming a time of computer printouts, optical character readers, central data processing, chips, and "the science of automated office mechanics." But the greatest game possible, the most exhilarating and consequential experience, is the adventure of confronting a potential donor with the opportunity of sharing in a great dream. If this book does not provide a precise road map, perhaps it does contain helpful directional signs and landmarks.

> *"I am sorry this book is not*
> *some other kind of book, but*
> *the next one shall be."*
> —Israel Zangwill

PART II

18
RESEARCH BEHIND THE BOOK

"We would often be ashamed of our finest actions if the world understood all the motives which produce them. There are countless actions and decisions which appear ridiculous, whose hidden motives are wise and weighty. Who knows, who can tell what truly causes the motivation to certain deeds. What thoughts and drives, what influences, what past experiences, what inner-most feelings motivate the action?"
—*Francois De La Rochefoucauld*
Maxims

THIS BOOK is a treatise on motivation. It is an examination of the impulses and stimuli that drive people to make large gifts. Really large gifts. It is the celebration of the inspiration, consideration, and lure that result in large gifts. Everything else in the book is peripheral.

When I first started this journey of discovery, I planned for the foundation of the book to be an expression of my own personal experience. This still remains a major focus of the material.

I felt, however, that I could not properly cover the subject without interviewing a number of men and women who had actually made gifts of consequential proportions. The sessions would be easy if I interviewed people I knew well, and reported faithfully what I had heard. I would reveal the truth and essence that motivates their giving. And just as importantly, I would uncover why they did not give to certain programs. But, what questions should I ask to ensure the most penetrating and productive disclosures.

I decided on a scheme to have professionals in the field, battle-tested professionals, help me in determining the format for my questions.

I designed a questionnaire listing twenty-two of the major factors which I feel motivate giving. I sent out several thousand of these questionnaires to fund raising leaders in seven different areas: health, education, religious, YMCAs, the Salvation Army, and cultural institutions. In addition, I sent questionnaires to those I felt were "qualified experts" in the field—consultants and professional fund raisers. I received over one thousand replies. A number suggested additional factors to those I listed, and quite a few wrote long letters regarding the material and their interest in the study. The response was excellent. And extremely helpful.

What evolved is a format and a listing of questions which could be used easily with the men and women who were the million dollar givers. I also asked those I interviewed to evaluate the factors.

The results are fascintating. I asked all those involved in the exercise to evaluate each factor on a scale of "1" to "10"—ten being the highest. Some variances are of interest.

The survey itself was not undertaken as a Promethean

audit of awesome intellectual proportions. Nor is it intended to represent a scientific and valid sampling. It was simply my attempt to understand more fully the attitudes of those in the field—and then compare those figures with the motivations the million dollar givers gave me.

A strong belief in the mission of the institution was by far the chief motivating factor indicated by the givers who were interviewed; it was also the major factor indicated by those who returned the questionnaire. A "great interest in a specific program within the project" rated second highest among those in the field. The actual donors rated this quite low.

Those in the field gave the next highest ratings to "is actually involved in the campaign program," "serves on the Board of Trustees . . . of the institution," and "memorial opportunity." The actual donors rated all three quite low.

The donors listed "belief in the mission of the institution" as their over-riding motivation and there was not a close second. Following that, they indicated community responsibility and civic pride," although in that item they actually took a more universal position—community representing the world as a whole. Third was "regard for staff leadership" sharing the spot with "fiscal stability of the institution." Actually, they tended to relate these two factors as being rather synonymous. This does not correspond to the attitudes expressed by those in the field.

It is revealing and essential to examine carefully these tables. We find that tenets we have held dear, and venerated, may not be motivating factors at all.

Of special note are several factors that donors evaluated openly and honestly. In the course of our discussion, however, it became obvious that their statistical rating did not relate to their visceral feelings. Take, for instance, the matter regarding the "recognition of the gift." This rated a low fourteenth on the scale. In actual fact, I am convinced that the appropriate and tasteful recognition of the gift is exceedingly important to these donors. Woe to the institution that has not developed a well defined program for recognition. In the book, I recommend the "Rule of Sevens." In one instance a major zoo did not properly recognize a donor for her major gift. When the donor made the gift, she indicated, with much protestation, that she did not want any recognition and did not feel that the major new facility should carry any name identification. The zoo acceded to her wishes and even failed to invite her to the opening of the new facility. She is now lost to them forever. Far better to push the question, encourage the donor, urge the recognition.

The "religious or spiritual affiliation of the institution" rated very low among the donors. In actuality, I found that in the case of most there is a deep and abiding spiritual quality to their giving. It is not necessarily "churchy" or for organized religion. But the spiritual sense is present and important. The institution should be quite aware of this when it seeks a major gift.

One phenomenon was present in every single interview. It was a factor I had not included in the profile and had not even thought of asking. Yet, it was discussed at length in each interview. Most often, the topic was initiated by the interviewee. Each donor spoke about the joy they experience in their giving. The magical and glowing ecstasy. Institutions, however, never sell joy and ecstasy. They sell facilities, equipment, and repairing roofs. Campaign material, the case statement, the carefully typed personal requests hammer away, point after point, at the specifics of the program. But seldom is there reference to the exhilaration and the joy. The evidence is clear. We in this business miss a consequential opportunity.

The tables provide a statistical base highly worthy of review and discussion by your institution's staff and volunteer leadership. It matters not one wit that the statistics may not be precise or valid for scientific substantiation. They are sufficiently accurate to provide a plan of desired action for your organization.

Every institution is different, unique unto itself. What is significant is the concordance of motivating factors. The similarities are inviolate, no matter what the organization.

It is fair to say, as many of the professionals in the field did, that no single factor plays the dominant, overriding motivation. It is indeed most often a serendipitous confluence of a number of factors. Still, settling for this thesis will most likely put you on the losing side! It is obvious that donors have a certain path they follow and there is a remarkable singularity to their rationale. Study this carefully, take it to heart. The results will never be less than exciting, and—more often than not—will be successful.

HOW'S YOUR R. P. G.* QUOTIENT?

Before you review the following graphs, take a few minutes to check the table that follows. Compare your ratings with those of "experts," other professionals in your field, and men and women who have actually made gifts of $1 million and over.

Think for a moment what you feel are the factors which motivate a person to make a major gift. We define "major" as any donation in the range of mid-six figures or more.

Weigh the importance of each factor in the table and score them, "1" to "10"—ten being the highest. Then, go to the Appendix and see how your evaluations compare with nearly 1000 others who have also checked the list.

*Reasons People Give

_____Community responsibility and civic pride

_____Tax considerations

_____Regard for the volunteer leadership of the institution

_____Is actually involved in the campaign program

_____Serves on the Board of Trustees, a major committee, or other official body of the institution

_____Has an adult history of being involved in the institution

_____Recognition of the gift

_____Was involved at one time in the activity of the institution—personal benefit

_____Memorial opportunity

_____Respect of the institution locally

_____Respect for the institution in a wider circle—region, nation, state

_____Religious or spiritual affiliation of the institution

_____Great interest in a specific program within the project

_____To match a gift or gifts made by others

_____To challenge or encourage other gifts

_____The uniqueness of the project or the institution

_____The appeal and drama of the campaign material requesting the gift

_____Fiscal stability of the institution

_____Guilt feelings

_____Regard for staff leadership

_____Leverage or influence of solicitor

_____Belief in the mission of the institution

APPENDIX

REASONS PEOPLE GIVE

Reason	0	1	2	3	4	5	6	7	8	9	10

Community responsibility and civic pride

Tax considerations

Regard for volunteer leadership of institution

Is actually involved in the campaign program

Serves on the Board of Trustees, a major committee, or other official body of the institution

Has an adult history of being involved in the institution

Recognition of the gift

Was involved at one time in the activity of the institution—personal benefit

Memorial opportunity

Respect for the institution locally

Respect for the institution in a wider circle—region, nation, state

Religious or spiritual affiliation of the institution

Great interest in a specific program within the project

To match a gift or gifts made by others

To challenge or encourage other gifts

The uniqueness of the project or the institution

The appeal and drama of the campaign material requesting the gift

Fiscal stability of the institution

Guilt feelings

Regard for staff leadership

Leverage or influence of solicitor

Belief in the mission of the institution

0 1 2 3 4 5 6 7 8 9 10

HEALTH

There were 387 responses from directors of development and those involved in fund raising programs in hospitals and medical centers

REASONS PEOPLE GIVE

	0	1	2	3	4	5	6	7	8	9	10

Community responsibility and civic pride

Tax considerations

Regard for volunteer leadership of institution

Is actually involved in the campaign program

Serves on the Board of Trustees, a major committee, or other official body of the institution

Has an adult history of being involved in the institution

Recognition of the gift

Was involved at one time in the activity of the institution—personal benefit

Memorial opportunity

Respect for the institution locally

Respect for the institution in a wider circle—region, nation, state

Religious or spiritual affiliation of the institution

EDUCATION

368 responses from college and university presidents, vice presidents for development, and directors of development

REASONS PEOPLE GIVE

Reason	0	1	2	3	4	5	6	7	8	9	10
Community responsibility and civic pride											
Tax considerations											
Regard for volunteer leadership of institution											
Is actually involved in the campaign program											
Serves on the Board of Trustees, a major committee, or other official body of the institution											
Has an adult history of being involved in the institution											
Recognition of the gift											
Was involved at one time in the activity of the institution—personal benefit											
Memorial opportunity											
Respect for the institution locally											
Respect for the institution in a wider circle—region, nation, state											

Factor	Rating
Religious or spiritual affiliation of the institution	6
Great interest in a specific program within the project	6
To match a gift or gifts made by others	4
To challenge or encourage other gifts	4
The uniqueness of the project or the institution	6
The appeal and drama of the campaign material requesting the gift	5
Fiscal stability of the institution	3
Guilt feelings	3
Regard for staff leadership	4
Leverage or influence of solicitor	6
Belief in the mission of the institution	8

RELIGIOUS

91 responses from a highly selective group of church leadership in the Protestant and Catholic Communions—mostly at national and regional levels. Several local congregational ministers and priests were added who had recently completed major campaigns.

221

REASONS PEOPLE GIVE

	0	1	2	3	4	5	6	7	8	9	10

Community responsibility and civic pride

Tax considerations

Regard for volunteer leadership of institution

Is actually involved in the campaign program

Serves on the Board of Trustees, a major committee, or other official body of the institution

Has an adult history of being involved in the institution

Recognition of the gift

Was involved at one time in the activity of the institution—personal benefit

Memorial opportunity

Respect for the institution locally

Respect for the institution in a wider circle—region, nation, state

Religious or spiritual affiliation of the institution

Great interest in a specific program within the project

To match a gift or gifts made by others

To challenge or encourage other gifts

The uniqueness of the project or the institution

The appeal and drama of the campaign material requesting the gift

Fiscal stability of the institution

Guilt feelings

Regard for staff leadership

Leverage or influence of solicitor

Belief in the mission of the institution

0 1 2 3 4 5 6 7 8 9 10

YMCA

The questionnaire was sent to the chief executive officer of the 90 largest YMCAs across the country. There were responses from 64.

REASONS PEOPLE GIVE

Reason	Value (0–10)
Community responsibility and civic pride	5
Tax considerations	4.5
Regard for volunteer leadership of institution	6
Is actually involved in the campaign program	6
Serves on the Board of Trustees, a major committee, or other official body of the institution	6.5
Has an adult history of being involved in the institution	5.5
Recognition of the gift	4
Was involved at one time in the activity of the institution—personal benefit	4.5
Memorial opportunity	4.5
Respect for the institution locally	6.5
Respect for the institution in a wider circle—region, nation, state	5.5
Religious or spiritual affiliation of the institution	5.5

	0	1	2	3	4	5	6	7	8	9	10
Great interest in a specific program within the project											
To match a gift or gifts made by others											
To challenge or encourage other gifts											
The uniqueness of the project or the institution											
The appeal and drama of the campaign material requesting the gift											
Fiscal stability of the institution											
Guilt feelings											
Regard for staff leadership											
Leverage or influence of solicitor											
Belief in the mission of the institution											

SALVATION ARMY

Sent nationally to the highest ranking officers in the Salvation Army. There were 24 responses.

REASONS PEOPLE GIVE

Community responsibility and civic pride

Tax considerations

Regard for volunteer leadership of institution

Is actually involved in the campaign program

Serves on the Board of Trustees, a major committee, or other official body of the institution

Has an adult history of being involved in the institution

Recognition of the gift

Was involved at one time in the activity of the institution—personal benefit

Memorial opportunity

Respect for the institution locally

Respect for the institution in a wider circle—region, nation, state

Religious or spiritual affiliation of the institution

Great interest in a specific program within the project

To match a gift or gifts made by others

To challenge or encourage other gifts

The uniqueness of the project or the institution

The appeal and drama of the campaign material requesting the gift

Fiscal stability of the institution

Guilt feelings

Regard for staff leadership

Leverage or influence of solicitor

Belief in the mission of the institution

0   1   2   3   4   5   6   7   8   9   10

CULTURAL

Questionnaires were sent to the directors of development and a selective group of executive directors representing the nation's largest museums, art institutes, and orchestra societies. There were 71 responses.

REASONS PEOPLE GIVE

Reason	Value (scale 0–10)
Community responsibility and civic pride	6.5
Tax considerations	6.3
Regard for volunteer leadership of institution	6.5
Is actually involved in the campaign program	7.2
Serves on the Board of Trustees, a major committee, or other official body of the institution	8
Has an adult history of being involved in the institution	7
Recognition of the gift	6
Was involved at one time in the activity of the institution—personal benefit	6
Memorial opportunity	6
Respect for the institution locally	6.5
Respect for the institution in a wider circle—region, nation, state	6
Religious or spiritual affiliation of the institution	5.5

QUALIFIED EXPERTS

"Qualified experts" is a subjective term. A list was developed of professional fund raisers, resident campaign directors, consultants, and officers of fund raising firms. There were 77 from this group who responded to the questionnaire.

REASONS PEOPLE GIVE

	$1 MILLION GIVERS	AVERAGE	QUALIFIED EXPERTS	CULTURAL	SALVATION ARMY	YMCA	RELIGIOUS	EDUCATION	HEALTH
Community responsibility and civic pride	8.1	5.8	6.54	7.88	5.00	6.42	4.77	5.11	6.15
Tax considerations	2.4	6.3	6.40	6.31	4.56	6.42	4.54	5.63	6.26
Regard for volunteer leadership of institution	6.7	6.4	6.76	4.88	6.01	7.04	4.15	4.60	7.01
Is actually involved in the campaign program	4.5	6.9	7.44	6.50	5.89	6.33	6.08	7.29	6.69
Serves on the Board of Trustees, a major committee, or other official body of the institution	6.5	6.9	8.11	7.25	6.50	6.83	6.69	7.89	7.10
Has an adult history of being involved in the institution	6.1	6.8	7.14	6.81	5.56	5.79	5.00	7.38	6.80
Recognition of the gift	4.9	5.9	6.03	6.01	4.11	5.00	4.46	5.54	6.18
Was involved at one time in the activity of the institution—personal benefit	5.7	5.9	5.86	5.41	4.56	6.25	4.23	5.73	5.99
Memorial opportunity	3.7	6.9	5.87	5.25	4.67	5.67	4.54	5.79	6.34
Respect for the institution locally	7.0	6.9	6.76	6.19	6.89	7.67	6.38	6.77	6.94

Respect for the institution in a wider circle—region, nation, state	5.47	6.27	6.46	5.13	5.88	5.94	6.19	5.8	6.2
Religious or spiritual affiliation of the institution	4.61	5.47	6.15	5.87	5.56	5.31	5.57	5.1	5.0
Great interest in a specific program within the project	6.84	7.12	6.38	6.79	6.44	7.07	7.53	7.6	5.9
To match a gift or gifts made by others	5.35	5.10	4.08	6.21	4.56	6.25	4.87	5.3	3.9
To challenge or encourage other gifts	5.36	6.10	4.15	6.31	4.00	6.13	5.90	5.7	4.5
The uniqueness of the project or the institution	6.13	6.20	6.00	6.33	4.78	6.31	5.82	6.1	4.6
The appeal and drama of the campaign material requesting the gift	4.30	3.87	3.46	4.04	3.00	4.02	4.11	4.1	2.3
Fiscal stability of the institution	5.89	6.70	4.77	6.96	4.50	6.01	6.49	4.2	7.4
Guilt feelings	2.95	2.32	2.83	2.96	3.88	3.15	2.30	2.7	1.3
Regard for staff leadership	5.32	6.43	4.00	5.86	3.25	4.75	6.08	5.4	7.4
Leverage or influence of solicitor	6.80	6.41	5.92	7.79	6.25	7.60	8.11	6.8	6.0
Belief in the mission of the institution	7.80	8.73	8.38	5.32	7.11	7.94	7.69	7.9	9.6
NUMBER OF RESPONSES	387	368	91	64	24	71	77		

TOTAL RESPONSES FROM ALL GROUPS—1082